Thankyou A
without y
this book
have been written
X

Housekeeping
for the Soul

Housekeeping for the Soul

Love, Cleanse and Protect Your Spiritual Self

Lorna Hedges

First Printing: 2017
ISBN-13: 978-1547122042
ISBN-10: 1547122048
Ray of Light Publishing
Gloucester, Gloucestershire,
United Kingdom.

www.rayoflight-teachings.co.uk/

Ordering Information:

Special discounts are available on quantity purchases by corporations, associations, educators and others. For details, contact the publisher at the above listed address.

U.S. trade bookstores and wholesalers please contact:

Ray of Light Publishing, email <PsychicLorna@Yahoo.co.uk>

Cover Design: Paul King

Disclaimer:

This information in this book is not intended as a substitute for consultation with healthcare or other professionals. Any use of the information herein is at the reader's sole discretion and risk. Neither the author nor the publisher can be held responsible for any loss, claim, or damage arising out of the use or misuse of any, or all, of the information contained herein.

Contents

----------------oOo---------------

Foreword

I have known Lorna Hedges since she was 16 (then known as Lorna Lester) and let me tell you, that was one heck of a long time ago! There was then a pretty large gap when I didn't see hide nor hair of Lorna, and in that time she met her husband, Andy, got married and had four children.

Lorna and I reconnected, via a Debenhams link (we both worked there as window dressers in the early 70s), on Friends Reunited seven or so years ago. What orchestrated our reunion, you might ask? Spirit did. I feel certain of that.

Back then, in 2010, Lorna was starting to do more and more psychic mediumship work and I was just coming to the end of my time in my first psychic development circle, before gingerly starting a circle of my own. Since reuniting, Lorna and I have worked together more and more, and now, with Lorna running various workshops, I am tasked with creating all of her graphic design promotional material, as I am a fully qualified graphic designer. I also lead Lorna's students through guided meditations. Additionally, we both work voluntarily offering Reiki healing and guided meditations at Charlie's, a cancer charity in Gloucester, on most Wednesdays.

In our lives, we are often, without even realising it, drawn to reconnect with people from our soul group - this is the case with Lorna and me. We trust one another, we inspire one another and we have a lot of fun together. What more could anyone wish for in a friend? Our very close friendship brings to Lorna's Thursday circle, of which I am also a member, the highest of energy, and because of this the evenings are always fun-filled and an inspired learning ground for all of the fortunate members.

This, Lorna's brand new (second) book, *Housekeeping for the Soul*, will gently take you by the hand and lead you along the pathway to true enlightenment. Trust me, I can sense it!

I wish happy reading and the highest of learning to you all.

Paul King Gloucester UK 2017
Author writing as Ed Newbery-King
DeMorte: Legend of the Lanes;
Do You Believe in Magic?;
The Collected Tales of Nathaniel Darcy

(magicgraphicdesignanddigitalillustration.co.uk)

Preface

I love my job. Yes, I do. I meet lots of lovely people on a daily basis. In my first book, *From Housewife to Psychic,* I explain what it is like for someone to become open to the world of spirit. This book explains how to protect the self inside and out from the rigours of our daily life.

I have been a Psychic Medium for about 15yrs now; not very long in layman's terms, but looking back I was always a bit different from the others.

There were so many things that happened throughout my life which this book could have explained to me, and maybe it could even have helped me put things right.

I have a beautiful family, but like most families of today, we had lots of ups but so many more downs. I am a wife, a mum and a grandma. My family are my life. I love them dearly, and they come first in all that I do in service of Spirit.

I had no intention of becoming a medium, but life took me straight down that path and knocked on the door to another world. It then took me into teaching about Spirit, so that all of a sudden I had help from my beautiful Spirit Guides.

Each week, on a Thursday evening, I hold a development group, but more people wanted to join and there was always a waiting list, so I opened another group every other Saturday. Then, to my amazement I opened a Meditation group once a month, which has also turned into a development group with meditation.

I also run workshops as a regular course for people who need more knowledge. It sounds very grand, but it is in fact hard work. As I said at the beginning, 'I love what I do', and I can think of nothing better than to be connected to Spirit and be daily helping people any way I can.

Of course there is the big 'I' in the equation and I would like to make it profoundly clear that it is in fact not me who provides all of this wonderful knowledge to all of the lovely people who need to learn, but to point out that the Spirit Guides who work with me are in charge of how this happens. They advise, they encourage, and they bring lots of beautiful love. I am the go-between who is in service to the highest.

Yes I need to be 'on the ball'; I need to understand what I am being told. They don't rule me, but I certainly couldn't do this all on my own, so the more help from the Spirit world the better.

There is always a need to know more. I am inquisitive, always looking for more. The answers may not always come immediately, but if the message comes across many times I get it in the end.

This book comes to you with love and I would like to dedicate it to my family. First to Andrew Hedges, my husband, for putting up with me for over forty years, as I'm not the easiest person to live with. Then to my children in order of age. Mark Hedges, my oldest and wisest soul; my daughter Rebecca West aka Bex, homemaker and teaching assistant to boot. Thank you for my beautiful grandchildren; Luke Hedges, my lovely son, who has had a hard time but is finding himself at long last; and my youngest daughter Elizabeth Hedges (aka Liz), who through trial and error stopped beating herself up and has grown into a beautiful woman.

To my good friends: Paul King whom I can go to with my troubles; Michael Doherty and Kelly Martin for taking my book and making it special; Amanda Dear (Sales Academy 2012) for suggesting this book as I try to ignore the Spirit world when they create more work for me; and lastly, to all of my beautiful people, too many to name, but you know who you are. I love you

all, and you make spiritual development easy to teach,
when you are all so receptive.

Therapist Principles

Just for today, I will disconnect from
other people's energy.

Just for today, I will protect myself with my cloak,
my bubble, and my shield.

Just for today, before every therapy, I will ask
for assistance from the celestial helpers.

Just for today, I will ask for there to be
a fair exchange of energy.

Just for today, I will cleanse all of my Chakras.

The Light Within

I was inspired to write this book by a lovely lady who approached me one day and told me that her friend was unwell through working with bad energy. She was emotionally drained and physically quite poorly. This can be due to repeated misuse of energy and not looking after the subtle energy field within.

Many years ago I quickly learned how to clear my subtle energy field, the Aura, and the Chakras, (all explained within the contents of this book).

She knew that as I regularly write workshops and teach from this method, that I could write a workshop for people who can help themselves from the inside out, a self-help workshop.

I thought about this for no more than 2 minutes and went home to start on the writing. A couple of days later, after thoroughly enjoying the feeling of putting something together that could make a difference, it was finished.

I also started observing many people in all walks of life, not just therapists but people who deal with negative individuals on a daily basis, who are struggling with their energy levels.

The workshop was a great success, and is still achieving more recognition.

The next thing that happened was that a lady approached me after one of these workshops and let me know that the next book I would write was going to be this one; she even gave me the title. Thank you Amanda Dear.

The challenge I had was putting a small workshop into a book that made sense, but was easy to follow. I have picked up books in the past that were so complicated that I went away feeling dismayed, as I can only grasp things that are explained in simple terms. It's the way I process everything.

I had a connection to my Guide and asked the best way to write this book based on a simple four-page workshop manual. It seemed to all come together through the Spirit world; everything just came in to my head without too much effort.

I never intended to write another book. My first book, *From Housewife to Psychic*, was enough for me. But this book seemed to be what people are in need of, to help them live life comfortably, without the negatives coming in every time a meeting of people takes place.

The difference being that we need not take on those negatives.

I am not bad at putting together workshops and writing up the manuals that go to make a brilliant course for my students. They gain so much from being given the knowledge that the Spirit world has been painstakingly trying to contact and inform many thousands of people for a very long time, but being able to put these workshops in a book format has been a challenge to me, so I really hope that when you read this book it will inspire you to feel differently about yourself and your family as you will be able to protect not just you but also them.

Energy is vibration. It is light; it is sound, and we are all responsible for our own energies, that which matters to you and within the surrounding energy.

We live life with our everyday experiences creating our own learning, our own dramas and the processing of other people's dramas. Who we are is our vibration and this governs how we act, how we interact, how we respond to life's little dramas. In a nutshell it's all energy, so use your energy wisely, because the more you give away, the more other people will just take.

I cannot express in words the feeling of love that comes from deep inside. My own connections to Spirit have been a most challenging journey, because getting it right is never easy. We should never judge ourselves or others when something goes awry. Always remember that everything that happens in life is a learning.

We can try to make this learning and growing through spirit a little easier by following some simple rules throughout our spiritual development.

Light has emerged from a deep connection to the Spirit world. It isn't a light that just automatically switches itself on. It's a light that has to be worked on day by day to get the right balance.

We all have this light. It is hidden quite deep inside, and to find this light, you need to be open to love, to forgiveness, to trust, and integrity, and that is mainly of the self, because if you cannot forgive yourself for any past hurt, who can you forgive.

I had always known deep down that there was much more to life than what we see through our three dimensional minds. There is another existence, the life that we cannot see with our physical eyes. It hides behind the third eye and reveals itself there as a picture when answers are needed through Clairvoyance.

It also comes as a flash of inspiration, which could potentially be a 'eureka' moment, a subtle feeling, or an urge to do something risky outside your comfort zone.

4

To achieve this light is about preparation, allowing you to receive from the universe. Getting the balance right is key to developing the light from within, and to feeling safe on all levels as the light around you grows.

It's as easy as brushing our teeth or washing our faces. We just have to learn how to; how to undo the negative thoughts, and to have faith and trust that love overcomes all harmful energy.

Energy

Energy is either Yang or Yin, positive or negative. We all carry energy in one form or another, and simply put, we are energy.

We create most of the energies within us and around us. We choose who we would like to be; we select a negative or a positive day, depending on our energy makeup, and if we listen to our egos, we are faced with a negative day, as the ego only comes from a negative energy. If we listen to and follow our spiritual side, we choose to have a positive day, as the spirit comes from a positive energy.

If someone around us is not very pleasant, they are pushing their energy onto us, and we in turn call upon the ego to help with this negative, thus creating more negative, even when we are not in reality thinking about it. Our thoughts produce our mind-set. We question things, and we pick things apart until our heads hurt from over thinking a situation. In short, we have then created our own negative energy. It is human nature to react to a negative with a negative.

In this situation never over think, just let go, especially if this issue does not belong to you, but if it does, then find the simplest solution to rectify those troubles, and let it all go. It sounds easy. It's not, but if we train ourselves to leave people's behaviours, actions, inventions and dramas alone, we are already half way to having a positive day for ourselves.

Nothing is easy through our human learning, but we could make our lives a much more pleasant experience.

Negativity

Negativity will always block the light, and then progression can be slow. It's inevitable in this human life to make human errors; after all we are human! Yet this will culminate in your light being temporarily obscured. It's pretty hard for a light energy to work in low, negative or dark energy.

There may be feelings of despair that can set in. Isolation can make us feel dejected, the complete feeling of being alone on this planet. These feelings are typical of someone who has stepped around the light into depression. The cause is negativity.

It all sounds far-fetched but believe me it happens, and the only thing that can really lift you out of this unpleasant sensation is to pull back into a positive frame of mind, but you need to follow a few simple spiritual rules.

It is not all doom and gloom. Once you have acknowledged that this negative energy could rule your life as it does through the ego, you are more likely to be able to set some ground rules for yourself.

Negativity will come through in many different forms. It can make itself out to be physical, the realness of something felt, and it can definitely be in the spiritual, in a low spiritual energy.

You will know when the negative energy makes its appearance. The feeling will force it's way deep in to the pit of your stomach (solar plexus). It will feel like a steam roller has just driven directly through you; it will feel horrible. As a result of it, you may feel very sick to the stomach; it may present as a headache, or you may get awful smells drifting around like a sewer is blocked, or an incessant itch that just will not go away, and the sensation of being unbalanced as you sway on your feet.

These types of energy can come in as spirit energy, maybe someone who was a mischief on this side of life, or someone who had a grudge to bear. They don't all turn into light beings that bring love. Some spirits can be downright rude. I would never be talked to in a demeaning way on this side, the physical life, so I can definitely say that any low spirit energies would never try to talk to me in that way from their side of being.

Then there is the manifested energy, the type that has been born from our negative human nature. This energy has happened because someone has formed it through their fears, blocks and negativity.

Maybe an argument has happened at home and you feel miserable. The negativity sets in, you feel terrible, you start feeling worse, then you start to see shapes or feel sick, the feeling gets bigger, and through this feeling you have just produced an energy which then feeds off your own fears. It's called manifested energy; it has been influenced by your negative behaviour.

Yes it happens, I have come across this many times. It happened just like that for someone close to me. In the end she thought that she had a ghost in her wardrobe. It sounded just like someone trying to get out by shaking the wardrobe and banging on the door to be let out, yet there was no one there but her own fears. She was the one who had created that type of energy, and it terrified her; not a nice occurrence.

However you feel about this experience, just look at it as a challenge; liken it to a nuisance; let go of the fear you create in giving it energy, and be open to getting it gone.

How to safely remove this energy

Safely removing a manifested (this is not spirit) energy is pretty well easy to eliminate. You just don't give it any thought; you have created it, so you alone can un-create it, by clicking your fingers, snap, and saying, 'Shrink'. Sounds daft doesn't it?

Well actually no, it's not that silly, it will go when you have decided that it does not and will not exist for you. It is after all an energy that you may have created or fed with your own fears, so let go of fears. These types of energy feed from all of your negative behaviours.

Dark Energy

To remove most dark energies, you may require a little bit more help from a professionally qualified medium who has worked in that field. Always go for someone who is reputable, and find out a little about how they remove an energy such as this. After all you don't want this force to grab on to someone and hide behind them. These types of energies have a tendency to try and hide in a corner somewhere on the property so that they don't get found out. They want to cause havoc; they want to be a nuisance, and some may be quite arrogant and think they can get the better of you. I will always thank them for coming in for the learning. This is courtesy, however malicious they may be as they are still living energy, not of this life any longer, but of another life. Even dark energy has a place in this world and the next, because we cannot have a Yang without a Yin. In other words, for every light there is dark; it is part of life and living, but these energies are there for someone's learning after all and they don't just pop by one day for no reason and just knock on your door. They may have been called in, or you may have picked this energy up whilst visiting a very dark, low or negative place. It happens and everyone needs to be more aware of this energy and be responsible.

Dark energy will just love to hide between the dust and the muddles. It is that place where dark really feels at home. I have nearly missed these energies when performing a house rescue. They go to the deepest darkest corner where you would not clear because out of sight out of mind is the best hidey hole.

So just remember to have a good clear out every now and then and just clean in the corners where the muddles have been. It will feel so much better.

Being able to connect with the higher energies

Before being able to connect to the higher energies, some ground rules need to be put in to place. These are laws that can help you through your spiritual growth and can help anyone on their own path to enlightenment.

It's not all love and light though, as you have seen in the previous chapter on negativity. However, you are the one who is solely in charge of your own personal energy, and never forget that. You have really just borrowed your physical body, but your true self, which is your higher self or soul, is the purest of spiritual energies.

Not only do we have to endure rules that have been made for our physical life, but also there are spiritual laws, the do's and don'ts which count towards your daily protection. Yes, these laws happen within the spiritual realm, and yes, some unusual energies can slip through, but effectively you are in charge.

Rules that are made on this earth are sometimes obstructing, whereas rules that are made via the spirit world are in place to help us here on this earth, so that when we pass over it does not seem like they are imposing anything on us, as it will always be for our greater good.

But remember that when the ego rules, the spirit will listen, but cannot answer.

When connecting to other beings that are not of this earth any longer, we should learn how to identify all energies especially whether this energy is either light or dark energy.

Some dark energies can make you think that they are all love and guidance, whereas in fact they can be those pesky manipulating energies from our own thoughts, or energy sent to you through malicious intent. This can be very confusing when these Spirit energies step in. Complicated I hear you say. The ego is pretty well ruling our lives from the negative, so stay positive if at all possible.

But we can all still live in harmony, light and dark, if we are to build a life here on earth. We just need to remember some of these simple rules, for how to safely remove an unwanted energy from either you or your home. It would be unwise to tackle this without advice from a professional, which is why you need to seek guidance from people around you, and I have found that word of mouth recommendation is the best method.

You would not roam the streets at night time without putting into place some sort of physical protection. That would be fool hardy.

Nothing is easy though, especially when you are just starting out on this fantastic journey of spiritual learning. It really is not all Scary Mary, but sometimes we reap what we sow.

I have loved every minute of my journey including the bad bits, as they have been there to help me recognise all of the good that is arranged via our spirit friends.

Of course we don't always make this negativity ourselves. It can be picked up from the ether, it is energy. It could be another person's energy, so in truth it does not belong to you, and this is why learning protective techniques to avoid these harsh realities is a pretty daunting task and the question is where to begin.

Reading on could give you the tools for when you are ready to connect with your Guides and Angels, or maybe just to keep you and your family safe and protected.

Defining the Energy of Spirit

You have an energy with you, but you are unsure of what or who this energy may be. There are ways to find out. Ask this spirit energy if it has come to you from a God source; ask if it brings the love from the God source, and then ask it if they love the God source as much as you do. If you hear a resounding yes to each of these questions, you will have a beautiful energy with you, and if it cannot answer, then you will have a dark manipulating energy with you.

You may not hear the answers. That's also okay. For each question asked, try to get the feeling from the pit of your stomach. If you feel happy with butterflies in your tum, then it's A-Okay, but if you ask these questions and get the feeling of sickness or a bulldozer has just rolled through you, then not at all okay. Easy peezy, yes, now you're getting the general idea.

Positivity

The polar opposite from the negative is the positive. When you are positive, you have a barrel load of energy to give away; you feel open and loved; you feel that someone in the spirit world is with you, as the hairs on your head, back and arms stand on end, giving that eerie feeling, the feeling of butterflies in your stomach (solar plexus), but this is a delight, or it is your light; not so far-fetched now is it? You feel alive and connected to life; you feel energetic and not tired out or switched off from life; you are in good spirits as they say.

You are switched on. This light is a power; it is energy and you feel ready to do business, but remember that this light can be blocked by negative activity just like that (click). Not permanently, just until you have your life in order.

So the answer is to protect your light, as there are far too many negative humans out there willing to share their negative energy. They can be called psychic vampires, a term that has been around for many years.

This book covers the practicalities; the 'how to' of protecting our personal energy field from the negative energy fields of other people, other life forms and other places. Negativity of any kind can be harmful to the human energy field (aura). Fear, anger, depression, negative people, places, arguments, and more in fact generate negative energy that can stick to you or build up in your home and cause inconvenience or worse. Spiritual cleansings are essential, for you and your home. I recommend that they be done at least every few weeks, more if you find you are feeling stressed or exhausted, or you are working on a daily basis with negative people.

When I work with people on a daily basis, either through Reiki healing or giving readings, it can have a physical influence on my life. It can drain my energy or it can boost my energy depending on how I protect myself. Protection comes with practice; it's like the right fit of clothing. If it feels comfy then use it, but if it doesn't feel at all right then the protection is not vibrating with the correct light energy for you. It's always going to be trial and error getting the energy to fit.

When offering Reiki healing therapy, there are many different energies that any therapist will connect to, and negative energy can come from the clients. After all they are coming to get a healing for not feeling great, and when they come along, they may have just had a major argument with someone in their lives, which can make their energy negative or low.

As a Psychic Medium, I pick up more on any energy, be it good or bad, and I have learned how to deal with these issues. This is part of the so-called job description.

It's not stressful in any way as long as you know just what to do. A good understanding of the 'how to' takes time, and if you can't wait to learn about energy, but have the awareness that something isn't right, then it probably isn't. However there will be plenty of different methods for how to look after yourself and your place of living or work.

I had given my life a lot of thought, especially about my spiritual growth, as I was open to all the energies, good and not so good, and what I was about to embark on, in my learning, would bring the dark and terrible energies my way, and of course, unless I fully understood about this dark unseen energy and all of the ghastly things that go with it, I would not be now writing this to help you.

In order to protect both me and my family my subtle energy field needed more than just a goodnight kiss. It needed to be nourished with love. Having developed my protection skills, I am now able to pass this information on. This was exactly what I did do. I had to learn from scratch how to, so that I could eventually impart this knowledge to you.

Researching Energy

I then researched different websites and asked my Guides to point me in the right direction to get as much information as I could. There was a lot of information out there, but of course it needed to be condensed, otherwise I would have spent nearly a whole day just trying to remember how and what to do to protect my energy field.

Explaining about energy can get extremely complicated so I hope to have put this in basic form so that everyone will understand the fundamentals. Energy is living; it is everything on this planet that is, or has been; it is life itself, it is everything that has been made, be it natural or man-made; it is plants, rock, sand, sky, stars, planets, sun; it is everything that exists in this and other Universes; it is life after death......it is Energy.

Getting it Right

Getting it right for ourselves daily, and I mean daily, not weekly or monthly, as every day brings with it new energy, and new challenges, it is important to our wellbeing, physically, emotionally and mentally.

Different energies can and will affect the whole self, whether you are a therapist, or a supermarket cashier. When dealing with people day-to-day, the energy will be either really fantastic with lots of happy people, or horrible with the awfully negative individuals coming into the aura, which will affect the way your day goes, and what you end up taking home after your shift or session.

We don't necessarily need to touch one another to feel someone's energy. It will be felt through the aura, so when we pass someone on the street and feel extremely sick, or even bubble up with laughter for no reason, this is the feeling that our energy body will pick up on that comes from our aura bumping into their auras (subtle energy fields). Also the sensation of going into a building and feeling intensely nauseous, or loving this feeling that you get from the place, this is the subtle energy field picking up on the energy of what is inside that building, good or not so good.

Energy Explained (Psychometry)

Just because we can't see it, does not mean that energy, either good or bad, doesn't exist. We create our own energy. We can pick up energy through the spiritual realm as well as the physical world. The force of energy, as we know it, comes in as a feeling. Energy is a vibration, so everything on this planet and everywhere else vibrates at different speeds. For example, your feet touch the earth and the speed of this energy lower to the (ground) is much slower than the energy at the head which vibrates much faster. This is because we are closer to the universal energy.

Everything in the Universe is energy and a lot of things can be altered with energy. Every person, every thought, every emotion is energy. Our subtle energy field is alive and intellectual. Anger will produce an unpleasant energy, whereas happiness will affect us in a very enjoyable way. This can only be good.

The auras (outer body), and chakras (inner body) can become blocked and distorted, but our total energy field can be purified with good housekeeping of the self and surroundings, allowing the self to become balanced, and healthy. Reiki energy healing is a method that I use to do precisely that, but there are many other ways to properly protect yourself, to cleanse the inner self and outer self.

Everything in your home or workplace vibrates. Our vibration can be knocked a little off alignment by the touching of an object that has been in a pretty unpleasant place, maybe bought second hand, or from an antique centre. The object or item may be vibrating with some horrible energy because of where it was placed.

Unsurprisingly, we may pick up this energy, which can expose us to the very energies we are trying so hard to get away from, and we have taken on that ghastly vibration.

The touching and feeling of objects is called Psychometry, the clear feeling of an object or photo or item giving the sensation of someone's or something's energy field, stored within the item.

This can be easily resolved, by sageing, which is the act of lighting Californian White Sage and with incantation or prayer , smudging the object.

Or if you have touched the item/object, and you have taken this energy in to your own body, you will need to ground this energy as soon as possible, and the best way to do this is to go outside and stand on the earth, and from the head push all old energies down to the toes into the roots (grounding. The old energy will be swallowed up by the Earth Mother. Then ask for the Angels to fill you up with their light and love. The feeling is pretty overwhelming.

More on smudging further on.

Energy That Moves

Negative energy can easily jump from another person's aura to your aura. Energy is alive, it moves around, and you can become affected by the negative energy of those people, places or objects, that you cannot avoid unless you wear armour every day, but there is always a solution to the problem.

Since it can make us feel physically ill, the energy then becomes real, it can be felt, and there are so many different ways to help with the healing of our subtle energy field.

We are all gifted with the ability to send out our individual energy field, our own being of power. We humans are energy transformers; we are alive and just beginning to understand how much of this collective energy we believe in and how freely it flows directly through us. The energy rays make a perfect pattern and maintain us, which manifests in opening a constant transference. Sounds pretty well complicated, but in truth, energy explained can be complicated until you feel it.

In other words the higher the frequency of energy that pulsates through our individual fields, the more we can feel it.

Imagine a low level jet flying just above the rooftops. The vibration and the noise is pretty powerful, and imagine the feeling of that without all of the noise. This is energy in the physical. Now envision this type of vibration that comes to you through the Spiritual. That is what many mediums, psychics, therapists and empath's feel. It is life itself, and we have all felt this within our life cycle.

Being empathic means that you are able to relate to how other people are feeling. So how is this different from being an Empath?

Empath is another term for clairsentient. With that, we're moving from the world of psychology to the world of spiritual feeling and healing. An empath will be highly sensitive to objects or items around them, and to people especially through their pain and anguish. An empath will feel the energy of the day, when there may have been a tragedy with many hurt. The empath will feel this pain, but all empaths should learn how to let this pain go, disconnect and send in the love, this is crucial so as not to constantly feel.

Dark, Low or Negative Energy and How to Let Go

Dark, Low or Negative Energy can be a bit like a fly on the end of your nose, and the best thing you can do with this fly is to flick it off. Fear of a dark energy may bring in a manifestation of negatives and low energy.

It can be unsafe to make assumptions and our approach is that everything is energy taking a particular form for a particular reason. Most of the time it can be dealt with, but it can be complex and first it must be determined what we are dealing with. Some energy requires healing before being released.

When you fear less and love more, protection is always around. Your guardians cannot reach you through the low energies from the fear that you are putting out energetically, particularly as it causes a block. This is internal, it is something which we take for granted, the goodness always being there to protect, but of course there is a big brick wall that they have stumbled up against, the negative you.

Dark or low energy is a nuisance, but can easily be put right with the right person who knows what they are doing. With the right words and the correct energies this can then be resolved.

Psychic attacks are defined as the manipulation of paranormal energies and forces.

Psychic attacks occur when negative energy is deliberately sent from one person to another person or place, causing instability in both the material and energetic bodies of that person or place. This negative energy can be called a spirit, an entity, a thought form or a dark negative energy. Each of these energies can create damaging effects within the person receiving them.

Of course, we have to also accept that this is happening. Many of us can brush away this type of energy flux as if we're just having a bad day, feeling pretty well rough, needing time from our daily hectic life style, etc. Of course this can also come from a physical nature, someone having a go.

The difference with this thought is that once these energies have done with us they will eventually skip to the next individual, so we must be responsible for our actions and our own subtle energy field, as there will always be a cause and effect situation. I would never wish a negative or dark energy on anyone. The consequences could be unspeakable.

An instance of bad energy coming into the home was when a friend of mine gave a lot of thought to the Fred West situation Being a Spiritual human being she overthought the circumstances and in doing so she went to her stairs and saw Fred West walking down the stairs in his spiritual form, thus creating the energy for his spirit to enter. (Fred West and his wife Rosemary were found guilty of at least 12 murders of young females between 1965 and 1985)

No, this in reality does not occur all of the time, but it does not help when it has been brought into the home through a negative thought process. The process by which negative actions affect a person's life can be quite complex. In the case of a psychic attack, there may have been nothing we could have done differently, other than not allowing this energy to enfold us, by following some simple laws of protection, but psychic attacks do happen, and they seem to be happening more often today or are we just able to define this energy much more.

Some dark energies and entities will find their way into our physical and energetic bodies. Some manifested energy can be sent without knowledge, even when it is sent by humans. Other energy that is sent deliberately to create harm and damage, is often to control, manipulate or punish the individual. This can entail ritual behaviour or the use of psychic powers , or a mixture of both.

You may actually hear some people say that negative energies and psychic attacks do not exist and cannot take place if you don't believe in them or if you don't give them energy by focussing on them. This is not true. I have met the biggest sceptics who have been under attack psychically. Trouble can and does happen as a result of negative energies and psychic attacks.

Auras are weakened by our negative beliefs, our negative emotions, and can also be weakened by the regular use of drugs and or alcohol. As a result, the care and protection of your energetic body is as important as the physical body, so that you can ward off psychic attacks and stay strong and healthy. After all you wouldn't go two days without having a shower or brushing your teeth. You look after your physical body so remember to take care or your spiritual one as well.

The Energy of Spirit

Connecting with the spirit world can be a challenge, but reading through many spiritual books will help you to develop your sixth sense. The key to a good connection is to meditate on a daily basis; this brings in relaxation and calm.

There are many of you who will be saying "I can't meditate, it's impossible for me, my head is all over the place".

It is not about shutting out the world; you would have to be a monk to do that. It is all about discipline, allowing yourself the time for you to not think about the outside influences that rule your everyday routine.

Trusting what is happening to you physically is paramount in getting it right, the feelings are beautiful, and the love is unconditional. Trusting ourselves is not something which develops without any problems. We humans frequently second-guess our beliefs, even our hunches and psychic experiences. We ask ourselves, "Is that real?" or, "Did I just make that up?"

The difficulty with self-doubt is that it acts to destroy all psychic abilities; much in the same way that unfailing self-doubt will destroy our greatest potential.

There are also many brilliant free guided meditations on YouTube and my suggestion would be to start with these. It is not always possible to shut out the world, but it is achievable to listen and use our concentration on someone else's voice.

Listen to Your Intuition.

Try listening to your intuition and see what results you get. Many people dismiss their intuition. Do not mistake your ego for your intuition. If you're hearing thoughts like, "Don't bother asking her out, she'll never go out with someone like you" then that's your ego. That is your negative side. Practice talking to your guides for ten or fifteen minute every day. This will help the answers to filter through easily as time goes on. It may not feel as if you are getting anywhere at the start, you just need to be patient and to let the process develop naturally.

Cord Cutting.

We're living in very spiritual times, even though it may not seem like it. There is change everywhere. We just need to be aware of this. We have cords attaching us to each other and to places, keeping us from being free to move around. You cannot see these cords, but they are there. Our energy can be drained through these cord attachments and we need to free ourselves from this draining energy.

It doesn't hurt anyone or anything to detach; it just frees us to give more love and attention to the people or things we detach from, and you can then give yourself and those around you more freedom.

It's no excuse that because you can't see it you're not responsible for it. Your energy is affected, and even controlled by your intent. So if your intent is to learn to clear it and stop throwing energy or accepting energy thrown at you... to stop allowing anyone to suck your energy (like a psychic vampire), then it will happen.

How many of you suffer from terrible headaches with no known cause, or perhaps aches and pains that may come and go for no apparent reason? Do doctors seem to be unable to help you? Sensitive people often have strange symptoms that clear up when they learn to take care of their subtle energies. Learn to clear your energy and learn to protect yourself from outside influences.

Illnesses (dis-ease) start in the energy field first. No, you may not be able to 'fix' every physical problem. But clearing your energy field cannot hurt you and will help you. Even if you have a constant physical problem, it can't hurt for you to take some responsibility for clearing and cleaning your own energy field. Cord Cutting is useful when you are attached to someone in an unhealthy way that negatively impacts your spiritual, physical, mental or emotional well-being. The Cord Cutting can release pent up anger, sadness or other strong emotions that may be attached to the cords. Oftentimes, you will feel lighter and more at peace.

Again you may need to ask for help with this method. If you cannot see the cord you may feel it, so imagine you have a cord that attaches you to most everything around in your energy field. See or feel this as an umbilical cord that protrudes from your solar plexus (tummy). You can ask Archangel Michael to help you cut free from these fears (this is all that the cords are). Ask him to sever the cords of fear with his blue light sword, and then send love to whomever or wherever or whatever the situation is. You should start to feel much lighter afterwards.

Emotional Cord Cutting

Cords are always formed out of fear, never out of love. They get thicker as relationships deepen through the passage of time. It is the neediness that strengthens them. The cords are usually attached to a major chakra point.

Negative emotions that come from the memory of past relationships and past events drain the life force from your energetic body, making you prone to illness or depression, or preventing you from moving on and experiencing peace in your mind and in your heart.

If the memories of your past experiences can still trigger anger, jealousy or pain in your present, you are still emotionally attached to them. These attachments are like metaphysical cords that can keep you stuck in the past, no matter how much you try to forget them.

During our lives we form ties to the people around us, to situations, places, habits, and events which are important to our sense of self. Most of these ties are positive and life affirming or important for our life journey, but there will be some cords which we 'hold on to', even though we feel that we are ready to move on. In the Emotional Cord Cutting process the Healer identifies the energetic form of these cords. Using a ritual they are then cut, the energy field sealed and healing energy administered.

These processes will repair your energetic body and leave you free to love again and move forward in your life.

The Unseen Force
and Who to Ask.

Whilst asking the unseen force of the universe for protection, we first have to accept that there is more than just this physical world. To have a belief does not necessarily take you into some sort of religion. It is what is in your heart, that is your faith.

There is an unseen place from where we arrived into this life from our existing home. We cannot see this in our physical form, but how wonderful it would be if we could.

It took me a very long time to work this out. I have a soul. This soul energy that never dies goes on for eternity. It is the purist form of energy; it is love, and as I sit here to write this, my soul is connected to every part of my physical body including my heart, and tears of joy are trickling down my cheeks.

I talk to Spirit daily, I ask questions, I get answers. This is something everyone can master with help.

When asking for help with protection, the hardest choice is to decide who to ask, especially if you have no belief system in place. My choice was made long ago. There is only one whom I can ask and that is God who is the highest form of energy. No, it is not a big man sitting in the clouds with white hair and a beard. It is an energy that makes my heart sing. This is pure love. We are all a little bit of God, all a little bit of that love.

Maybe you believe more in the Angels. That's ok. Say your prayers or affirmations daily to the Angels. You may believe in the Ascended Masters. There are too many to write them all into this book, so go online and search Ascended Masters. When one jumps out at you, direct your thoughts to that one and they will step in.

Or just maybe, you have no belief at all in all of the above. It's ok to worship the ground, nature or in this case Mother Earth. The energy is still in everything and all energy from the earth mother is listening. There is always the Sun and Moon energy, which are strong forces that work to bring in the highest of healing, but remember to direct positive thoughts always.

The energy in any case will be absorbed and end up in the right place.

Take little steps along your journey and discover whom or what you would like as this unseen force of protection.

What Do We Ask For?

First I ask God for there to be a 'fair exchange of energy'. I deal with people daily, who come for a reading or a healing, which means that some of my energy is being used to help either verbally or physically with hands on healing. Of course I always ask for the energies of light to step in and help with the energy before I start, which facilitates the God energy I have asked for.

Remember you may get what you ask for in many ways, so be careful not to criticize anyone when they are asking for help. This is bad energy and will only end poorly. Direct your thoughts to positive vibes , which will assist in the energy being happy and healing.

I have now put into place a vibration that allows me to give of both my energy and source energy, but I have asked this to return once the session has finished. I then ask for the angels or celestial beings to assist with this situation, either to send lots of love and/or lots of extra healing once I have finished.

We talk to ourselves all the time in our own heads. We tell ourselves off; we praise ourselves up; we ask for help.

'Let there be a Fair exchange of Energy'. Ask and ye shall receive.

Grounding

Why Is Grounding Important?

Grounding is a technique that helps keep someone focussed in the present moment.

It will at times feel like you are very much ungrounded. You will feel light headed, a muzzy head, maybe a little lost, nauseous, and dizzy, with the feeling that you have a job to put two feet on the ground, or that you are walking between two worlds, and total confusion.

As your awareness shifts into the new energy, your body can get left behind. If you can, spend time in nature to help ground the energy within as you too reach higher frequencies.

Grounding protects the body from becoming weighed down with universal energy and from being damaged if such overload happens. It's important for you to meditate and for you to make sure that some part of your body is on the ground making contact with Mother Earth.

Housekeeping for the Soul

If your situation means that you cannot contact the earth directly, you can visualise such contact in your imagination. The mind doesn't differentiate between reality and imagination.

If you are sitting in a chair meditating, try to not cross your legs and make sure both the soles of your feet are touching the ground. Then make sure that your spine is straight. No Slouching! When you have done those three things, visualize white coloured roots coming out of your feet like the roots of a tree. Spread these roots out deep into the ground all around you. This will make sure that you stay grounded.

Remember to meditate daily if possible, which will help with your visualisation when you need to cleanse quickly.

There are other techniques to grounding. If you do not feel you can meditate, eat something, take a shower, go for a walk, lie down on the grass, do some gardening, or just walk barefoot.

Whatever the choice of grounding technique it will feel right for you once completed.

Touch Can Facilitate the Sharing or Stealing of Energy

It can be difficult to protect yourself from someone who is constantly touching you to suck your energy or to poke at you. It's similar when someone gets very close to you, invading your personal space. That's what it can be – an invasion. The trouble is we all need to touch in some way, which is why we need to protect our subtle energies.

It can be very difficult when our work involves touching. You may be a healer, or a nurse, or you may work in a shop and you have to touch someone to take their payment.

Whatever your work is, it will probably involve touch, and even if you don't work, you will still be in contact with someone at least once in a day, unless you're a recluse.

We are connected in many ways through touch, but do we want to take on someone else's mood for the day or even week? If I had a reading booked in and my husband had come to me with a demeaning remark that makes me angry, this would definitely impact on the healing or reading and be passed as energy on to my client Blissfully, I never allow my husband to impact on my mood.

Of course, it is not just about touching another person. We can pick up energy from items of furniture, nick-nacks, and other paraphernalia. Just about everything has energy. If you go to a hotel and it's full of old furniture, you can guarantee that these objects have old energy stored in them, which may be good or it may be bad. (More on Psychometry later)

We all touch items all the time. How many of you will go in to a shop and pick up an item of clothing and love it when you see it, then change your mind as soon as you've picked it up? Chances are, you and many other people have picked up the same item thus putting energy into this piece. No, we can't go round all the time not touching and feeling items and objects. It's not the way of human nature. We are naturally curious mortals and need to feel.

However, you can learn to protect yourself from this energy by altering the psyche of thought, ask for the protection, see in your mind's eye a lovely colourful cloak or bubble around you, and feel the Angel protection come over you from head to toe. Simple things save you from so much negative energy, and it's only a thought away.

Soul Feelings

The soul is energy in its purist form. The force of energy is always with us, it came in at birth. Some say it arrives at conception, others say it arrives at the birthing. I say the soul arrives when ready to take on the human life.

The soul comes in to learn from our human existence, which could be good or it could be not so good. It depends on the soul knowledge and what it needs to discover.

This soul has been here probably a thousand times before. It may be finishing the learning and will want to go home. Personally, I get a longing to see my real home again, but I am in no rush as I have so much still to do.

As the soul learns, it gains knowledge of everything the human life goes through, so when we feel down or depressed the soul is feeling exactly that, and when we cry the soul feels that also. But when happy we feel in love with life and the soul will feel this, so when a medium says this spirit has gone home to rest, that is exactly what it has to do, to find the loving energy once more.

We can ask our soul energy to help keep us safe and protected every day. The power from this force will always be there to help us in our pursuit of life learning. Give your soul a chance, for this energy is part of you; you are as one.

Chakras

The Seven Chakras Explained

We have seven energy centres called chakras. They are energy wheels, and I like to think of them as lotus flowers with closed buds that open to become beautiful flowers that spin.

When we are well physically, emotionally and spiritually, these lotus flowers are fully open and spin at the correct speed, but when we are 'out of balance', some of the chakras may be partly open, and some may be totally closed. Balancing the chakras helps to correct the energy body, promoting good health.

The chakras are the colours of the rainbow, and are located in a line from the base of the spine to the crown, the top of the head.

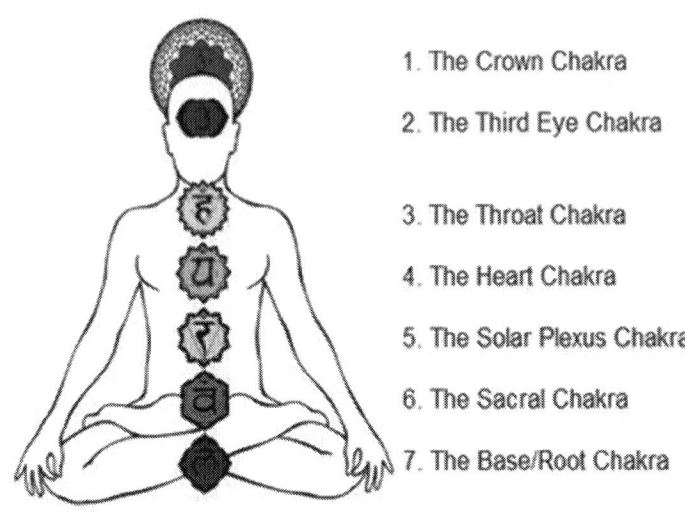

1. The Crown Chakra
2. The Third Eye Chakra
3. The Throat Chakra
4. The Heart Chakra
5. The Solar Plexus Chakra
6. The Sacral Chakra
7. The Base/Root Chakra

1. Crown Chakra. Top of Head. Violet

2. Third Eye Chakra. Above and between Eyebrows. Indigo

3. Throat Chakra. Base of Throat. Blue.

4. Heart Chakra, Centre of Chest. Green.

5. Solar Plexus Chakra. Just Above Navel. Yellow.

6. Sacral Chakra. Just Below Navel. Orange.

7. Base/Root Chakra. Base of Spine. Red.

Root Chakra

The root chakra at the base of the spine, is given the colour red.

Located at the base of the spine and red in colour, the root chakra is the slowest moving and governs our survival instincts, adrenal glands, skeletal system, legs, knees and feet.

A healthy root chakra connects you with strength to your family. When the energy of this Chakra is distorted it will function in a different way. Problems of survival such as emotional dysfunction, stress, anxiety, and restlessness can impact on life.

The health issues associated with the root chakra include joint pain, lower backache, obesity, constipation, and anorexia.

Sacral Chakra

The Sacral Chakra, just below the navel, is given the colour Orange.

In a relationship with the opposite sex, blocks in this second of the seven chakras bring lessons on jealousy, betrayal, control and power plays.

The health issues associated with the sacral include uterine or bladder problems, sexual difficulties, impotence, lack of flexibility, sciatica, lower back pain, and problems with the large intestines.

Solar Plexus Chakra

The Solar Plexus Chakra, located in the tummy just above the naval, is given the colour yellow.

The third chakra will pay tribute to our emotions, warmth, academic understanding, and self-confidence.

It is at this chakra that balance is possible. It is an energy point that brings in feelings of self-worth.

Blocks in this chakra will cause fear of negative reactions, the need to exert power over others, hot temper, demanding and blaming, judgmental attitudes, feelings of lack of appreciation, unfriendliness, fear of something new, low energy, uncertainty over which direction to go, and low self-esteem. It is here we learn of self-empowerment, integrity and self-respect especially of the self.

The health issues associated with the solar plexus are diabetes, hypoglycaemia, gallstones, nervousness, low energy, muscle cramps, stomach problems, lumbar spine, and liver disorders.

Heart Chakra

The Heart Chakra, located directly in the middle of the chest off centre from your heart , is given the colour emerald green.

When the chakra of the heart is open, we are able to forgive others including ourselves, our lungs will be clear and our immune system healthy.

A heavy heart is one that carries anger and irritation from deprived feelings and emotions, as well as guilt. To have a healthy heart, you must allow these dormant emotions to surface, heal, and then fall in love with yourself. An unhealthy heart chakra causes alone feelings and depression and affects how you love yourselves, and how you love others.

The heart lessons are self-love and forgiveness of yourself.

The health issues associated with the heart are high blood pressure, breathing difficulties, circulation problems, shortness of breath, chest pains, disorders of the heart, tension between the shoulders.

Throat Chakra

The Throat Chakra is given the colour Blue.

A healthy throat chakra creates a voice that is clear, and resonates with truth. The throat chakra is the power of changing our thought into word, listening as well as taking some accountability for our every action.

The blocks with this chakra make it hard to communicate, because we feel we are being swallowed by our emotions and feelings.

When the voice is weak, our truth plays a huge part in the performance of the throat chakra.

The health issues associated with the throat are fever, ear infections, weariness, thyroid problems, disorders in the throat, ears, voice, neck, cervical spine, and oesophagus problems.

Third Eye Chakra

The Third Eye Chakra, at the forehead between the brows, is given the colour Indigo.

A healthy third eye gives us the power to observe the reflections from the outer world, as a direct call for us to accept them as ours, heal and love them.

The blocks in this chakra cause us to become dull and unsympathetic, and to have poor memories.

Worry is a big problem. Feeling spaced-out and poor concentration will also afflict a person with a sick third eye chakra.

The health issues associated with the third eye are headaches, eye problems, pituitary, pineal gland and neurological problems.

Crown Chakra

The last one, the Crown Chakra, situated at the top of the head, is given the colour purple.

The force from the universe makes its way into our energy body through the crown, and moves down through the other energy centres to the root chakra.

Because we have a strong connection to an influence greater than ourselves, we feel through our crown the power bestowed upon us via the source energy.

Any blocks in this chakra cause bewilderment, depression, fear of success and lack of inspiration.

Auric Field

The auric field or 'Aura' completely surrounds the physical body and is as much a part of us as the physical body itself. The Aura vibrates with a higher frequency then that of the physical body.

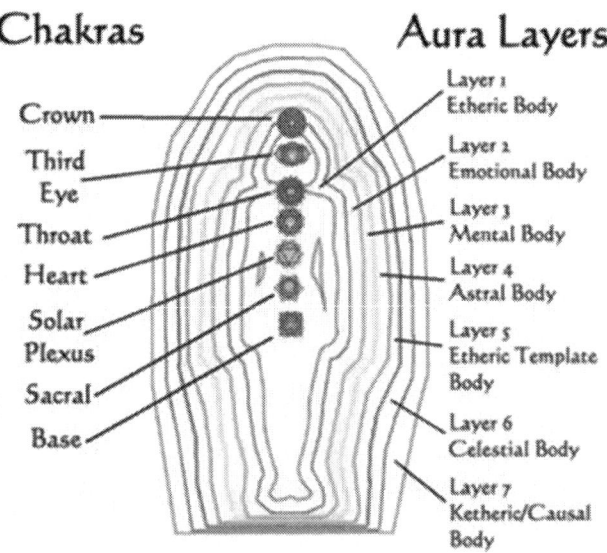

Chakras

Crown
Third Eye
Throat
Heart
Solar Plexus
Sacral
Base

Aura Layers

Layer 1
Etheric Body

Layer 2
Emotional Body

Layer 3
Mental Body

Layer 4
Astral Body

Layer 5
Etheric Template Body

Layer 6
Celestial Body

Layer 7
Ketheric/Causal Body

Aura

I'm sure you have heard of the electromagnetic field, which is a part of everything on this planet. This includes; humans, animals, plants and rocks. When we look after our own subtle energy field (Aura), which is connected to our chakras, spirituality and goodness begin to flow throughout our lives in a happy, pleasing way. Things that would normally have worried you, will not have such a big impact on your life anymore.

The Aura is made up of seven regular layers, each of which has a distinct frequency.

The Aura is formed by the energies given off by our chakra centres, and each person's aura vibrates with a frequency which is affected by any distortions in the energy of the individual chakras.

Just remember that any interactions of energy can take place all the time, everywhere you go and with everyone you meet. So it's essential to recognize how this development works in your daily life, how the energies are exchanged, and how the energy will affect you.

Meeting someone who has an aggressive stance, or who carries a lot of negative energy, or just by being near to them, can affect your energy body, because it's easy to soak up their energy. It can and will affect you in many ways.

The feeling of impending doom, a lack of understanding, being unreasonable and irritable are all part of taking on someone else's energy through the auric field.

All of this can lead to physical and mental health problems, giving rise to disease.

The layers relate to the physical, mental and spiritual bodies. Energy is vibration, so thoughts and feelings from hanging on to someone's problems, or even your own, will impact your health.

The outmost layer of the aura can extend to between five and seven feet from the body, but this will depend on the general health and wellbeing. Someone with a strong connection to Spirit can project their energy out much further.

The aura and the mind send signals to each other continuously. This energy radiates from our physical form. It gives out an image of the true self. The aura gives off a colour representing our mood, and our physical, mental and emotional health. Frayed edges may appear; colours may change; dark patches may show; due to our over thinking and bad health.

The Seven Layers of the Human Aura

The main seven layers of the aura are connected to the seven chakras.

The aura is the imprint of our physical, mental, emotional and spiritual bodies as a whole, with each layer reaching out to the next, totalling seven layers that we can define as human. I am sure there must be many more which we have not tapped into as yet, but for now we go with what we have.

The aura is a very important part of our subtle energy field; it defines how we feel, physically, mentally and emotionally, all depending on where we are or what we are doing in our day. This then will have an impact on our main chakras.

For instance, if someone has said something really bad to you which can be gut wrenching, that energy goes straight through your aura directly into you solar plexus (stomach). The overall effect will be, can't eat, feeling sick, stomach going into spasm.

This why we protect our subtle energy field. Protection needs to be from the outside to protect the inner self. The closer we get to the outer layer, the seventh layer, is where the protection needs to be; it needs to surround our subtle energy field.

The First Layer: the Etheric Body

The first layer is called the etheric body. It follows the physical outline of the body.

It extends about half an inch to three inches from the outer skin. It has information concerning our physical health. It connects first and principally with our first chakra, the base or root chakra, which connects to our organs, glands and meridians, (meridians are energy lines throughout the body,). It relates to the wellbeing, existence and protection of the physical body.

Physical illness and damage can be seen in and around this layer. The etheric layer is a most important part of our immune system and normally appears to our visual sight as a light blue or grey light.

This can be the easiest layer to see and is the first layer seen.

The Second Layer: the Emotional Body

This layer transmits to our feelings; the emotions within us and all emotions we feel for others around us.

The emotional layer may be seen as a rotating mass of energy around the body. It extends about one to three inches from the body and holds the emotional feelings. This is the means through which we will experience feelings as well as life.

It is chiefly connected to our second chakra (the Sacral Chakra). Continuously changing, the second field of the aura reflects our present mood.

This field can appear fairly murky when negative feelings and emotional blocks are there. Problems in this layer can have a negative impact at some point in the third and first layers.

The Third Layer: the Mental Body

The third layer is known as the mental body. It stores and runs agendas associated with our essential belief system, our intelligence, personal power and understanding.

This is the layer of thoughts and ideas. This layer is usually most visible around the head and shoulders as a yellow glow. It is in this layer that thoughts and ideas in fact become established Itis usually quite easy to see and will really stand out when you watch someone thinking or concentrating.

When connected to our third chakra (Solar Plexus), it extends anywhere from three to eight inches from the body. It holds our thoughts, ideas and mental development. Both the conscious and unconscious minds are energetic and never rest unless we are meditating.

In this layer, ideas and thoughts are updated and authenticated.

The Fourth Layer: the Astral Body

The fourth layer is called the astral body, which spreads out about a foot. It is connected with the heart chakra, creating and building the energy of love for people around us as well as the world.

If the first three layers of our aura mirror the physical character and presence, then this fourth layer is the porthole to our spiritual life. It marks the separation between the physical layers and the elevated layers, and coordinates between the physical & spiritual being. It is in charge of the interaction between people. It is the layer of love and of relationships, with others, yourself, and with your physical body.

The Fifth Layer: the Abstract Body

The etheric pattern is the fifth layer, extending about two feet outward. This aura connects with the fifth chakra, sound, communication, vibration and creativity. This layer is the spiritual part of us created at the beginning; it is part of our DNA makeup, which is our unique individuality.

The etheric body is a copy of the physical body on a higher level. It is the basic pattern of your individuality and inner character and serves mostly as a carbon copy of the physical body on the spiritual plane.

It represents the heavenly spark and allows our Higher Self to function within the person.

The Sixth Layer: the Celestial Body

The sixth layer of the aura mirrors our subconscious mind. It is known as the divine layer and extends about 2 to 3 feet from our body. This layer connects to our 6th chakra, the Third Eye. It is where our physical mind comes into a union with our spiritual mind through service to a commitment and through meditation. We got to this state through meditation and internal work, and understanding that there is actually no separation between other life forms and us.

This layer also holds the knowledge of having a connection to something much greater than ourselves. It is the body of the emotional level on the spiritual plane. It's the layer of collective awareness, clairvoyance, and the level of communication with other beings.

The Seventh Layer: the Ketheric or Causal Layer (The Soul):

This is the last layer that our human understanding is aware of, and is called the causal or ketheric layer. It can expand to over three feet which surrounds and holds all other layers together.

Vibrating at the maximum frequencies, the seventh layer mirrors all the knowledge and events that our souls have undergone, either in the present lifetime or in past lifetimes.

The ketheric layer is the link to divinity, God, Source, Creator, or All That Is and to becoming one with the universe. This layer signifies the Divine within us all and our connection with divine beings.

This is the mental layer of the spiritual level. It is our spiritual pattern. Through this layer we bond and grow to be one with Spirit, the element that never dies, but just evolves to more advanced levels.

Through this layer we can access the universal knowledge which has memory of any past existence both physical and spiritual.

The health issues associated with the Crown Chakra are migraines, brain tumours, coma, amnesia, nervous system and muscular system disorders, mental issues, and skin disorders.

The seven main Chakras impact our health. If you have had a bad tummy and it has been going on for days, the likelihood is that your solar plexus (tummy) Chakra will be spinning abnormally and not at the correct speed.

The energy centre needs help. We need to understand how to repair our Chakras on a daily or even weekly basis. There will be many meditations online through YouTube. Find the one that resonates with you. Search for Chakra Cleansing where you will find hundreds to choose from.

I will however give you my very favourite meditation for cleansing the chakras in the last chapter of this book.

Animal Protection

Yes even animals. We have animals in our lives right now that would do anything for us with such unconditional love. I have a dog that really would not hurt a flea, but 'if push came to shove' he would look out for me. This is a comforting thought.

He is of course a pet here on this earth still, but we also have those pets that have crossed over and are still willing to step into an earthly fracas, and they will make it known that they can still look after our earthly needs.

A power animal is a different energy. This energy may not have had an earthly life, but it would have sworn to protect you no matter what. It can be very empowering to connect with these power animals.

Meditation is always the best course of action. Just think of a lovely wooded area with an open space deep in the wood. Go there in your mind's eye and ask for your power animal to appear, but just be aware that we don't all have wolves or bears. You could see a dormouse and this may seem very funny indeed, but this little animal could have more energy than the big bear you were expecting.

Housekeeping for the Soul

Acknowledge your power animal and be grateful for this creature who comes to your rescue, which can be in the physical life or the spiritual life. Either way the energy will protect.

Get to know your animal protectors. They could impact your life in a big way.

Crystals

There is a wealth of knowledge online about crystals that could take me forever to write about, especially if it's for a particular ailment, mental physical or emotional. But as we are looking for a more specific crystal for protection I will start with the main one that I use and would recommend for anyone to carry around with them at all times.

Something pocket sized is perfectly adequate. The bigger the crystal does not mean the better the protection. No, any sized crystal will be good. It will still vibrate with the energy for your needs. Remember that if you carry this crystal around and programmed it with intention, it will work for you every time.

Crystals are unique in vibration; they are all vibrating at different levels, and they are known to give relief for certain medical conditions.

Of course wearing Crystals will change your vibration, an example being that if you have a pain in your hip and you place a *Lapis Lazuli* crystal in your pocket this can change your vibration thus lessening pain.

But a word of caution. Wearing crystals near your head, maybe earrings or a necklace, could give you a headache, depending on the type of crystal that you used. Or carrying too many crystals can make you feel quite sick when you are not used to the vibrational energy, especially when you are not grounded.

The crystal that helps me to protect myself and my home from negative low energy is a *Black Tourmaline*. For me this has to be the daddy of protective crystals. It has worked for me, particularly in my field of Psychic Mediumship.

When I go to a house clearing, I make sure that I have one in my pocket, although I did go to a house one time and found that after moving on a very naughty spirit with pretty low energy, I had to leave my crystal behind for the owner, as he attracted low energy spirit into his home.

I don't think he consciously went out of his way to say, 'Come here and haunt me'. It just happens to some people. I would hope that he uses it frequently as I have never been called back.

If you feel a little unloved or you have had a hard day and just want to wash away all of the negative energy, the best crystal for this is *Rose Quartz*. Pop a couple of tumbled stones into the bath with your favourite oils, then bathe and relax. This crystal washes away the rubbish and replaces it with love.

Another that has worked for people that I know is a practice that has been used for a very long time in the Feng Shui tradition, which is to place a piece of *Citrine* in the furthest left hand corner away from the front door of your home, and place a *Smokey Quartz* point, pointing at the *Citrine*. This is meant to usher in money with the *Citrine* and keep the money coming in with the *Smokey Quartz* . Another way to keep love in the home is to place a piece of *Rose Quartz* in the furthest right hand corner of the home away from the front door.

Some other good crystals for protection are:

Amethyst, for space clearing,
Fluorite, for mental clutter, and negative thoughts,
Moss Agate, for instability and grounding,
Tiger Eye ,for mental clarity and protection
Carnelian, for renewing your energies.

These are a few examples to help you to get a clear meaning of the power that crystals hold. Again, online there is a mass of in-depth info that will help you.

Please remember that these crystals take on yours and other people's energy. They need to go outside on the ground to recharge. As they originally came from the ground, the ground is the place where they will heal.

When using a crystal for the first time, you should programme the crystal with clear intention, so hold onto it for a few minutes, then with positive words ask the crystal to work for you to achieve whatever your wishes are, so for example:

I hold the *Black Tourmaline* and I then ask it to work for my greater good and all who hold it, to protect me on all levels. This means I have asked that this crystal protect me on the physical earth and in the spiritual as I work with spirit all of the time. There is nothing complicated in making your intentions clear.

Holistic Therapies

There are many different holistic therapies to choose from now. Not only is a therapy good for your emotional physical and mental wellbeing, it is also good for the therapist.

There are codes of conduct that therapists must follow. You should ask to see certificates of excellence, diplomas or NVQ pass grades.

They should also have Medical Malpractice and Public Liability Insurance.

It is usually a good move to get 'word of mouth' recommendations when choosing whom you go to for the first time. It can be a big decision when picking out a therapy that suites you.

Don't forget to protect yourself when meeting anyone new for the first time. Even therapists can have a really bad day. Why do you think that someone is coming for a therapy? Their wellbeing is down to what you as their therapist can offer emotionally, mentally, and physically.

Alexander Technique

The Alexander Technique works through assisting a person to improve the perception of their posture and movement. This may result in a better understanding of their balance and coordination, helping to improve functioning and their reactions to stimuli. In a typical Alexander Technique lesson a teacher will explain, and use gentle hands-on guidance, to help an individual find ease and balance in their simple movements and everyday activities such as sitting, standing, walking or bending. Alexander Technique may help people find relief from unnecessary tension and its effects. This can help to bring about a positive sense of well-being.

Aromatherapy

Aromatherapy is the therapeutic use of essential oils to help deal with everyday stresses and emotional well-being. Essential oils, extracted from plants, are thought to possess distinctive properties, which may be used to improve overall emotional and spiritual health imbuing the user with a sense of relaxation and calmness. In a typical aromatherapy session, the therapist will ask questions about previous medical history, general health, wellbeing and lifestyle. This helps the practitioner to choose and blend the safest and most appropriate essential oils for the individual. The oils may be applied in combination with massage or the therapist may suggest other methods.

Aromatherapy may be found to be helpful to those wanting to reduce everyday stress and so help with the ability to cope, relax and sleep. As well as being used in individual therapy sessions and at home, it is also used in a variety of settings, including hospitals and hospices.

Bowen Therapy

Bowen Therapy is a soft tissue remedial therapy that involves the therapist using fingers or thumbs to move over muscle, ligament, tendon and fascia in various parts of the body. This therapy can be effective to help relieve everyday stresses and revitalise the whole person. Each Bowen therapy session varies according to the particular problems of the client. By focusing on the lower and mid back and legs, the upper back, shoulders and the neck, a sense of wellbeing can be achieved, helping relaxation, aiding sleep – helping to remove everyday stress and anxiety that can make us feel under par or prevent us from functioning at our optimum.

Healing;

The history of Healing stretches back for thousands of years. Nowadays most healers view their work as a natural and purposeful energy-based process which, from mostly anecdotal evidence, is believed to help relieve everyday stress, provide a sense of physical and emotional revitalisation and on some occasions bring about a deep sense of peace. Each healing session will vary according to the needs of the client, but there are some general themes. The client remains fully clothed and may be seated or lying down. In simple terms, healers work with a conscious intention to help and support. The process focuses on using the hands, placed on or above different areas of the body, often in sequence, in order to facilitate a natural sense of wholeness and wellbeing. Although there are some variations amongst healers as to the philosophy and belief systems associated with it, most agree that healing recognises the sanctity within the holistic nature of being.

Hypnotherapy

Hypnotherapy is a skilled communication aimed at directing a person's imagination in a way that helps elicit changes in some perceptions, sensations, feelings, thoughts and behaviours. In a typical hypnotherapy session the hypnotherapist and client will discuss the intended alterations or therapeutic goals desired. The hypnotherapist will ask questions about previous medical history, general health and lifestyle to decide on the best approach for the individual. Hypnotherapy may be found to be helpful for those seeking relief from a range of problems and is used alongside a person's own willpower and motivation to seek a desired goal. It is often used to help relieve anxiety, aid sleeping, and help to address bedwetting, address attitudes to weight, and help clients achieve behavioural change to stop smoking. It may also help with minor skin conditions that are exacerbated by stress and confidence issues, and may also be used to enhance performance in areas such as sport and public speaking.

Hypnotherapy may help people to cope with and manage the relief of perceived pain.

Massage Therapy

In all types of massage therapy, the intention is to relax the soft tissues, increase delivery of blood and oxygen to the massaged areas, warm them, and help the body to relax. In a typical massage therapy session, the practitioner will discuss symptoms, medical history and the desired results. The practitioner generally performs some evaluation through touch before beginning the massage. Oil or powder help reduce friction on the skin and the therapist may use other aids, such as ice, heat, fragrances, or machines. Massage may be found to bring relief from everyday aches, reduce stress, increase relaxation, address feelings of anxiety and tension, and aid general wellness. It can also be used in support of other therapies to assist in the rehabilitation of muscular injuries.

Acupuncture

Acupuncture is based on the belief that small well-defined areas of the body, such as the hand, foot and ear, correspond to all organs and parts of the body. Evidence shows that stimulating these areas, usually with needles, may help to deal with symptoms such as anxiety or general stresses. In a typical acupuncture session, the practitioner will ask questions about previous medical history, general physical and emotional health, as well as medication, drug use, diet and lifestyle. Treatment generally involves the stimulation of defined points on a distinct area of the body using a variety of techniques such as acupuncture, electrical stimulation or pellets. Acupuncture is commonly used in a variety of healthcare settings, including hospitals, prisons, drug rehab units and complementary health clinics alongside medical treatments.

Naturopathy

Naturopathy is a philosophy and holistic healthcare system that recognises the healing power of nature present in all living things. As an holistic system it aims to promote and restore health by employing various natural treatment approaches that may include: naturopathic nutrition, lifestyle advice, hydrotherapy, physical therapy, naturopathic psychosocial support and other appropriate techniques. Naturopathic practitioners interpret presenting symptoms as the individual's unique response to physical, emotional, environmental or genetic stress factors which can be identified by asking about your family history. The practitioner's role is to identify these underlying causes and to promote the inherent self-healing power within the individual.

Nutritional Therapy

Nutritional therapy is the application of nutrition science in the promotion of health, peak performance and individual care. Nutritional therapy practitioners use a wide range of tools to assess and identify potential nutritional imbalances and to understand how these may contribute to an individual's symptoms and health concerns. This approach allows them to work with individuals to address nutritional balance and to help support the body towards maintaining health. Nutritional therapy is recognised as a complementary medicine. It is relevant both for individuals looking to enhance their health and wellbeing, and for those with chronic conditions wishing to work with or 'consult' a nutritional therapist in collaboration with other suitably qualified healthcare professionals. Practitioners consider each individual to be unique and they recommend personalised nutrition and lifestyle programmes rather than a 'one size fits all' approach. Practitioners never recommend nutritional therapy as a replacement for medical advice and always refer any client with 'red flag' signs or symptoms to their medical professional. They will also frequently work alongside a medical professional and will communicate with other healthcare professionals involved in the client's care to explain any nutritional therapy programme that has been provided.

Reflexology

Reflexology is a complementary therapy based on the belief that there are reflex areas in the feet and hands which are believed to correspond to all organs and parts of the body. Some practitioners may also include work on points found in the face and ears. Reflexology works on an individual basis and may alleviate and improve symptoms such as everyday stress and tension. During a typical reflexology session the therapist will take a detailed medical history. Sessions are usually performed in a comfortable chair or couch. If it is to be performed on the feet, the client will be asked to remove footwear and socks but other forms of reflexology require no removal of clothing. The practitioner will make a visual and tactile examination of the area to be worked before beginning the precise reflexology massage movements. The particular types of movements involved require the application of an appropriate pressure using the thumb and fingers. Reflexology can be a wonderfully relaxing experience where you can take time out from everyday pressures. The therapist's expert touch will help you relax which can help improve mood, aid sleep and relieve tension. The result is an overall sense of wellbeing.

Reiki

"Reiki" (ray-key) is Japanese for 'universal life energy', a term used to describe a natural system to help bring about an improved sense of wellbeing and a positive feeling of spiritual renewal. This tradition was founded by Dr Mikao Usui in the early 20th century and evolved as a result of his research, experience and dedication. It is a tradition that is open to any belief system, and benefits may include deep relaxation and the promotion of a calm peaceful sense of wellbeing. The method of receiving a Reiki treatment from a practitioner is simple. The recipient remains clothed and comfortably lies on a couch or sits on a chair. The practitioner gently places their hands non-intrusively, on or near the body using their intuition and training as a guide. There is no massage or manipulation. Reiki can be used on the person as a whole, or on specific parts of the body. It is also possible to receive Reiki at a distance. Reiki is taught by Reiki Master/Teachers, who have trained in the tradition passed on, in person, from Master to student. Students go through a process of initiation/attuning to the Reiki energy. They are then able to treat themselves and others, not only from a personal and emotional perspective, but also as an aid to individual development and spiritual growth.

Shiatsu

Shiatsu is a touch based therapy that applies pressure to areas of the surface of the body through loose comfortable clothing for the purpose of promoting and maintaining wellbeing. A Shiatsu practitioner will initially consult with the client and plan the Shiatsu treatment. The client will then be positioned comfortably, with appropriate adjustments being made throughout the session. Clear and accurate aftercare advice will be given. Shiatsu is a Japanese word that literally means finger pressure and derives its theoretical and practical roots from the ancient traditions of Oriental medicine. Today it is an autonomous treatment method influenced by Chinese, Japanese and Western knowledge. In addition to being regularly used by thousands of people all over the world, a variety of charities, health foundations, NHS trusts and hospitals in the United Kingdom provide Shiatsu to support patients whilst receiving treatment for a range of health issues and to help them maintain their general wellbeing.

Yoga Therapy

Those who wish to develop their natural wellbeing may find yoga therapy a useful route. Yoga therapy is taught by yoga teachers with additional training and experience in the therapeutic adaptation and application of yoga. People may be taught one-to-one or in a therapy group setting. Yoga therapy may help with many issues and can be appropriate for a wide range of ages and lifestyles as well as those looking for a healthier way of life. All that is needed from the participants is the desire to help themselves and the willingness to practise regularly. Through practising a yoga therapy programme, the participant may, for example, become more aware of posture and breathing. She/he may also find that regular practice can help to promote relaxation, aid sleep and relieve tension; it may help to contribute to an increased sense of wellbeing and a positive mood. In a typical first yoga therapy session a medical history will be taken by the yoga therapist. The body, posture, simple movements and the breath may be observed and issues and concerns discussed. Working with yoga therapeutically is about the whole person. The yoga therapist will then assess how yoga therapy may help before planning and teaching a practice tailored to the needs of that individual. Practices may include one or more of a range of techniques such as posture work, breathing, relaxation, working with sound, reflection, and/or meditation. A number of sessions are likely to be needed to confirm safe and appropriate practice.

Of course these are only a few to choose from. Believe me there are hundreds more.
(Descriptions taken from Complementary & Natural Healthcare Council)

A Fair Exchange of Energy

Before each reading I always ask the Source for a fair exchange of energy, which means that we ask for the highest energy to step forward to help us, while not giving away too much of our own energy. There are times when we just give of ourselves, so the need to ask for a safe return of our precious energy is acceptable. It's that or feel tired out at the end of the sitting.

So now you know how to feel safe with your Guides, Masters and Angels, it is time to make a connection.

This feeling will come in as pure love. You could not mistake what you are receiving. It is a feeling of never being alone or even lonely; a feeling that everything will be okay; an emotion which gives you the need to cry out loud with passion. It is, in its purist form, the energy of Spirit.

Being a Psychic Medium

The challenge I found many years ago was in understanding how to balance my work life with my family life. I chose to drop everything that I knew and pursue the unknown. I knew absolutely nothing about becoming a medium; all I knew was, that I felt different. I no longer wished to stay in my previous job, and I felt a calling.

It's not easy to give up what you know is safe and follow the urge to do something that does not make a proper living.

So learn I did, but the knowledge that was the most essential was learning how to protect myself from the onslaught of the people who thought I was cracking up, and learning how to ask for protection from the spirit world when I became very negative through listening to everyone who thought I was 'off my trolley'. This was a physical energy which I had to learn to deal with physically.

When dealing with the different energies, I ask for protection on all levels. I am covering all bases then, giving my celestial beings the information that I would like protection on this earthly plane and in the spirit world. As I work on both levels it seems impractical not to ask.

This was my biggest challenge. I had to find the highest protection to take me into the light, away from this negative depression.

I deal with dark energy and I also walk in the light, the beautiful feeling of unconditional love which is so intense. When I am in the light energy, this is my prime protector. The dark is poles apart from the light energy. The protection is different. I have a protector from the dark side that also helps me from the spirit world, but physically I carry crystals, I smudge with sage, and I place my invisible cloak on.

I not only work with the Reiki energy when healing, but also with the spiritual energy when giving a reading.

When Uncle Billy comes in from the world of spirit, and had suffered with bowel cancer when in this life, I really do not want to feel his illness for too long. After all, it was awful for him, and I am not unsympathetic to that feeling, but perhaps it could be for a short time to get the message over.

Some of us can wander round with a pain in our hip region, and the first thought is, maybe it's arthritis , or I could have twisted it without knowing, I'll make an appointment to see the doctor first thing in the morning. Then you are sent for an X-ray and nothing is found that the doctor can see, and it occurs to you that Great Aunt Mary had a hip replacement and that she was in so much pain a year ago when she died.

Of course she just wants you to know that she is really OK, so she stands next to you and gives you her pain. This is called Clairsentience, the feeling of spirit. All she needed was to let you know that she's fine now, and when you acknowledge this, the pain goes away.

Not all illness or pain comes from spirit. It can sometimes be our pain, so remember, if you are not sure go to the doctor anyway.

Do you have a room in your house that feels heavy or stagnant? Have you been through a major life change and you're feeling trapped in the past? Are you now ready to let the energy flow again and clear any resistance to abundance or change?

Another way for clearing is through smudging.

Smudging

About smudging with sage. This is a vital tool in the spirit cupboard, and your nearest new age or spiritual shop will have some, or you can buy online. Sage can come in stick form or pieces. You either hold the stick or place the pieces in an abalone shell. If holding, be careful as bits that are burning can break off, so a tin or saucer underneath is always a good idea. Light them in the usual way and waft the smoke with a feather. Ask for Californian White Sage when purchasing, and if using for the first time make sure you follow instructions, as you really don't want to burn your house down.

When using Californian White Sage, remember to open doors and windows otherwise the house will fill with smoke. Light the sage and allow it to burn for a few seconds. If the flame does not go out blow it out. The sage will smoke. Say an incantation or prayer that suits the situation, and ask for all negative low energy to be taken out with the smoke through the open doors and windows. Smudge every part of the workplace or home, and this will take the old energy out and bring in the new.

Some ideal (or essential) times for you to sage smudge your aura and/or space would be:

When moving into a new living place, home or flat.
When you start a new job or open your own business.
Before and after a visitor comes into your home.
Before and after a healing session is advisable.
Before meditation (optional)
After an argument or even after an illness

How Do You Connect With Your Guides Directly?

Wouldn't it be great if your guides could just call you on the phone and tell you what's coming in your future, or tell you to look out for a man named Steve, or that your children need you urgently and you should get to them right away? For some people that's nearly how it works. It just takes time and practice to be able to hear, see, or feel your guides. Here are some ways you can work on increasing your connection directly.

Making the initial contact with your guides can be a challenge. You need to be able to recognise their energy. It's a little like a signature; it becomes quite unique to you.

Spirit guides are not the entities that the film world would like you to believe. They are more than that; they are your right hand. We start to rely on them for their wonderful advice. (No, they can't give out the lottery numbers). They are with us to help us on this very challenging life journey.

They are not allowed to tell us what to do; they can only advise in a special way. I'm not sure I would want anyone else to tell me how to lead my life anyhow.

To feel that deep connection, you must first be in the zone so to speak. To be able to connect with your Spirit Guide is a privilege and an honour, and once a message has come through we need to learn our manners and thank them, as they have used a vast amount of energy to relay the message.

We can mistake our own voice in our heads for thinking that we have not made a connection, when in fact Spirit does not have a voice. They come in purely as a vibration, a light energy. Given that fact, your guide is merely using your voice to convey the messages.

Always remember that if you hear voices telling you that you are fantastic, that you are going to become a pop star and make lots of money, you need to take this message with a pinch of salt. It really means that you will probably have a low energy around you that needs attention, so don't allow yourself to give it any.

Asking the correct energies to step in and take away this entity will help to rid you of this nuisance. Like a fly on the end of your nose, just flick it right off, and always say thank you for the learning.

A pure guide will never control you or judge you in any way. The difference in the energy will be noticeable as a strong feeling. Your truest highest guide from God will always bring in so much love to you that you will become very emotional. That is the difference. They will advise if you ask, but they will not tell you what to do.

The vibration of the words that our guides bring to us can quickly feel supportive. They will always be honest with you; they do not hesitate, so when you start to doubt yourself, remember how you feel. Is this your ego or your higher-self allowing you to experience these feelings?

Automatic Writing

Another method of connecting to your guides is through automatic writing. This method allows you to just sit quietly and write what comes to mind, but of course, you will need to ask questions. If they feel they are worth answering they will help you to write this message down.

Of course if you ask them the question, 'Am I wearing red knickers?', you may not get the answer you want as you truest, highest guide will not feel that something so trivial needs an answer, but also keep in mind that if you do get a response to that question you may have invited a low energy in that wants a little bit of fun, which may not be to your liking as the mischief makers in spirit can be a nuisance.

So light a small candle and ask that your truest, highest guide step forward to bring messages of guidance through writing. Say a prayer or affirm to the Angels that you are protected, then ask your questions. The answer may not come straight away, so just be patient and sit quietly until the answer is there.

If you do not like the answer and you ask for the guides to bring in the answer that you want, again you may invite a low-level energy into your aura. Your guide will have already given you an answer; they will not give you another one for your indulgence.

Origins of Spiritual Awareness

I cannot say how far back we have been practicing mediumship, as the only evidence that is documented goes back to Victorian times, when séances and Ouija boards and cards were used as tools to help the medium.

There are still many people who use such tools, and no matter what is said through the Ouija board, you cannot guarantee that it is someone you know, and it could be a dark, negative energy. Anyone can answer a question in the spirit world to gain your trust, but then anyone who is a mischief-maker can also come home with you after the reading where such tools are used.

There was so called evidence of photographs taken showing ectoplasm, a sticky substance from the ether of spirit.

Ectoplasm, A so called strange, supernatural material that flows out of a medium's mouth during a séance.
This mysterious material would sometimes take the shapes of faces, limbs, or even a complete figure, but could not become visible until it had come out of the body of the medium.

There were those certain few who have attempted to contact the dead that date back in early human history, with mediumship becoming popular during the 19th century.

With professional mediums, they are the channel. They will have to ensure the bringing in of spirit and make absolutely sure it is a spirit that is known to you. After all you don't want just anyone to step in and give false information, and the medium will bring only true messages from the highest energies.

Being a Psychic and Healer

I had been a Psychic Medium for many years, learning all the basic knowledge and a bit more in protecting myself, my family, and my home.

Even I can still succumb to the negatives if I do not adhere to the actions needed to be a good therapist/medium. As there are numerous negative energies that come through my door on a daily basis, it is a complete must for me to literally go by the book......this book.

There are a variety of energies that come through my door, including people who are looking for a reading, and people who are in need of a healing. I had undertaken many years ago to work in service of the light or higher energies, the source energy.

My home has been equipped with a healing room to receive many people for therapy or readings, and I also teach from this room two development groups and several workshops every year.

It can be fairly well full at times with many people in and out and it's my job to make sure that these energies do not stay put. Not only did I have to learn clearing of the workplace, I had to learn clearing of my energy field or reap the consequences when the day had finished.

Different Energies

There are many differing energies, from negative to positive, the light and the dark, that have all been in my home at different times of my spiritual growth.

It's not just learning how to deal with the energy; it's about knowing if we have one of these energies with us that we try to be more aware of. Who or what could be invading our space is our learning.

How do we really know what is surrounding us, in our home or on ourselves. This energy can be picked up with a physical feeling, and the symptoms may present as nausea, dizziness, headaches, pain, itching, or bad smells. These are the many different negative or even dark energies that invade the self or place.

We can become easily stressed in our daily job life. Workplaces are not what they used to be; there are targets to reach, i's to dot, t's to cross; and it can get very fragile, making us feel under pressure.

The best course of action to alleviate the load is to bring a little light into the job. Cord cutting is a simple method used by many to let go of places, people and situations that get unbearably heavy.

It's not about letting go of a person and never seeing them again. It's about letting go of the fear, the negative energy built up over a period of time. We need to let go of the personal fears which trap us, which give rise to many physical ailments.

Places, events, people, everything has a cord. It's an attachment to something not healthy; it is in effect our ego built from our fears.

Our other concern in life is our family life. Perhaps you don't get on with Mum or Dad, and they may not be there for you, or you may be in a difficult relationship, where arguments are common and you just want for it all to end. When this energy exists in your life, it will not leave until you have rectified the situation.

Sorry is a big word; we do not say it enough. It helps to shift unwanted energy away. It can be really tough at times. We kick ourselves so much for the negative things that happen, but do we do anything about these unwanted energies that have materialised. We want more than anything for our relationships to work out, so we need to stop creating the anger and upset; we need to stop blaming others for our mistakes, and we need to learn how to say sorry.

This is meeting the negative energy half way to letting go of it

Ask for the positive energy to enter your being and to bring a more productive relationship with the people who are in your life. You can say this in a prayer form, or just affirm with as much positive verve as possible. Remember you are in charge of how this happens.

Mirrors

Some hold the belief that mirrors are the reflection of the soul, and when you see your reflection, you see the dark side of the soul. This is a belief that may or may not be true. I don't hold with this idea.

But we do all keep mirrors in the home, and there have been times when I have visited places where there is a large mirror hanging, very old and very ornate, yet there have been things that were not very nice hidden in this object. I do feel that mirrors can be a gateway to other worlds, a portal into another dimension.

Personally I think that as long as you keep your mirrors polished and clean on the outside, whatever may be hidden there cannot look back through because of the glare from the mirror's cleanliness. I also keep a cross on the back of each mirror to put the loving Christ energy in, and every now and then I polish the mirror with Rose Quartz water from a spray bottle.

A mirror is a powerful psychic tool. It can bring the user hidden knowledge and clairvoyant ability and can act as a gateway to other planes of existence. So only ever use a mirror with good intention, as this is another tool which can bring benefit, BUT also dark energy. You can never fully know that you have not inadvertently gone to the astral plane or another low dimension when scrying.

Scrying is defined as the art of gazing into or upon a crystal or dark mirror, allowing the physical eyes to relax and letting the inner psychic eyes begin to open to receive desired visions or information.

Feng Shui

Feng Shui, the Asian way of coordinating a home for the best source of positive energy, has a lot to say about mirrors. Using mirrors to visually expand a room and bounce more light into it also fills it with favourable energies. If there are any areas in the home where the energy gets trapped or doesn't flow properly, a carefully placed mirror can help redirect the energy to a more productive flow.

You do not need to have a deep understanding of Feng Shui principles in order to effect Feng Shui in your home. There are lots of easy Feng Shui tips you can apply right away to build a better quality of energy.

Starting out, it is helpful to recognize which areas of your home will need help the most. For instance, you might feel very good about your kitchen and your living room, and be inclined to spend quite a bit of time there, but your bedroom, bathrooms and your cupboards are ignored.

In Feng Shui, the house is observed as a whole being in which one part is simply connected to the other.

Ask for White Light

I tend to ask daily, once in the morning and when I go to bed, for protection on all levels, (in this world and the spirit world). This is important to my family and to me, and I need to get it right as I work in the energy every day.

People may be finding life really hard. There are too many choices these days and life can become extremely stressed.

Every morning I ask the highest source (God energy), to protect my family and me on every level with white light, and in my mind's eye I begin to see the light shining from the universe on all of my family and me.

I then ask for the highest guardian to protect my home with a golden pyramid of light. I can then visualise a golden pyramid coming down to surround my home. It's as simple as that and the more you get this right on an everyday basis, the better your life will turn out to be. It's not rocket science; it's everyday change to give a more rewarding and positive outcome to your day.

This is necessary for my work day, otherwise it can get a little overcrowded in my home with spirit energy, negative energy, and manifested energies, which can unintentionally come from my clients when they are going through so much pain and negativity, so asking for protection every day is a habit I have put in place for the comfort of me and my family.

I am still a Mum, a Grandma and a wife, and there is not a day goes by without complications and believe me, there can be many of those when I just ignore the signs.

I love working with spirit energy every day. It is part of my life, but I try not to let it take over as I need my feet to be firmly planted; I need to stay grounded.

Don't forget that you can protect family, friends, animals, and places by asking your celestial helpers on a daily basis. Say the words in a positive way. Any words will do. Just improvise, as long as it sounds good and always say thank you, after all they are doing their very best to keep you safe, but do remember that we all have free will, so they can only help us up to a point without our permission.

Herbs

Placing certain herbs around the home can bring in protective elements.

Fennel seed is very powerful at repelling negativity in all forms, so place some in a small dish to neutralize negativity.

Sage is brilliant for clearing away negativity, and it has cleansing properties that can be helpful in house-clearing rituals. You can purchase sage "sticks," which are small bundles of dried sage leaves tied together, which you can light and allow the smoke to "smudge" away any negativity in your home, or any other location. Remember to always ask permission if you are lighting sage in a place other than your own home.

Bay leaves can help you to strengthen your psychic abilities, repel negativity, and increase your personal power. Some more herbs are: Lavender, Cinnamon, Peppermint, and Basil. All with healing properties, and negative clearing.

There are so many ways to protect your family, yourself, your home and your workplace. Not everything may work for you, or maybe it will all work when you interchange protection methods. It only matters that you are safe from the negatives that this earthly life has placed upon us.

Pick out the bits that seem to be right for you; give yourself time to take it all in. Rome wasn't built in a day. This has to be gradual. You will more than likely forget some of what is in this book - that's also okay. You will use a technique that will fit into your daily routine that will be easy for you to remember.

Just keep in mind, that if anything does not work at any given time, it may well be your learning, but in the end you can only protect your person if you are true to yourself. Love is the strongest of healers and not much can break through those barriers, so send love to everyone and every place including you.

The Light

We have talked about the influence of dark and the devastating effect that this type of energy has within our lives. Now I must talk about the light.

You may not see light, but my goodness you will be able to feel it. Light is a part of you, it's inside, and when you dig a little deeper you can find this light.

Light feels happy, it feels amazing, and it will feel like everything in your life is going right for you in the most miraculous way, but we can often spoil this feeling by saying, 'This will never last', or 'It's my lucky day, tomorrow it will all change'. These words may usher in the negative, so be careful what you say as the universe is listening.

Feel the light and you will feel the best you've ever felt. It gains strength from love, the kind of love that you should be giving to yourself, the self-esteem kind of love, the self-confidence; this is what light feels like.

The ego will be stepping into our light allowing us to start on the negative cycle again. Ego can destroy; it is a negative energy and light cannot shine through the negative (yin).

We are all in charge of how we set our dialogue, but we cannot be on top of this dialogue every day, as it's part of our learning, but some of us hang on to our learning much longer than others, which can render us into depression, dark moods and lack of interest in life.

Meditation

So we've covered most things throughout this book, and I feel that this last chapter needs to touch on Meditation.

Now I hear you all saying, 'But I've tried and can't meditate. My mind is going round and round and just won't stop'. The bad news is, you've already talked yourself into the 'I can't do this for the life of me' attitude, but the good news is, it's all down to structure, brain training and patience.

If you don't succeed, try again until you do. Of course, it won't happen overnight. Being able to meditate can take time and you will know when you are able to meditate properly because messages come, pictures may come, feeling definitely comes. It's all about how to. This is where the internet comes in, the good old internet, so go and find some guided meditations which will help you with your healing and connections. It will help you to define the different energies. It's going to take time, but it is so worth the trouble.

The thing that helps to enhance this awareness aspect is meditation. It's through a relaxing, calming, meditation that we learn how to still the mind and, more importantly, to focus the mind. When we learn to focus the mind, we can learn very quickly the difference between our own thoughts and higher thoughts.

It becomes a routine of connections that pictures or feeling can become part of your reality, but in your head and body.

So if you start to meditate and the pictures are strong, like a dream in full colour, write it all down, because it can be messages from the Angels. If you don't get pictures, please do not give up, because you may be Clairsentient, (Clear feeling). I rarely get any pictures at all as everything comes to me through feeling. It directs itself through my tummy (solar plexus), and turns into a thought form which then wings it's way to my third eye where there may be a little show that goes on, but never that clear. However, this does not stop me from getting the gist of the message or understanding the meditation that comes in.

Again, go on to YouTube, and you will find many types of meditations on offer. Some can be a bit hit and miss, but sooner or later you will find the right one to suit your everyday needs.

Our emotions have a direct influence on our bodies, and with the way we feel inside and out. Of course, this may be why you might have discerned that the health of other people can be affected when they are stressed out. They can become depressed for quite a long time.

Anxiety and stress are one of the main reasons for poor health. It can be more noticeable in the form of diabetes, hypertension and other such lifestyle diseases, and it can also be apparent that a low or negative energy could be hanging around.

Meditation is a wonderful healer. We need to quietly meditate when we cord cut, or when we heal our Chakras. To be able to go through the colour spectrum of the Chakra system will help with healing the self, and if this does not work for you, then maybe it's time to seek advice on why you are feeling poorly. If the doctors can find nothing wrong, then you need to speak with someone who is able to pick up on an energy that may have attached itself to you. So if Great Uncle Billy had bowel cancer and all you have been feeling for the past month is pain in the lower abdomen, then it is a possibility that Uncle Billy is trying to get your attention. Again it's the Uncle Billy syndrome.

I visited a young lady for a reading way back. She told me that she suffered frequent migraines. It can mess up your whole life when you feel poorly, but if this is energy that is trying to get your attention, that is how they do it. Your guides mean you no harm, but sometimes it's the only way they can get your attention.

This young lady had a relative who had died from a brain tumour, and who was trying to get her attention. This is what was causing her migraines. As soon as he was asked to leave and to take the pain with him, the migraines stopped altogether. She is open to the spirit world but has not developed her intuition, so she was unaware of what was happening. The migraines could have stopped months ago if she had but known.

Meditation is the key to our wellbeing. When we meditate, the mind becomes calm and relaxed. It helps release worry from the mind, and tension from the body. Consequently when the mind is quiet, the emotions become balanced and the results of this balance show up as positive changes in the body.

There is no reason to think that meditation is hard going. We need not go into a trance state to get what is needed. We can sit and contemplate, because just being able to have a quiet moment can sometimes do the trick.

We imagine, we create, we heal. It's all within our makeup, and it's how the imagination works.

The Lighthouse Meditation

Please ask for someone to read this to you, and then close your eyes.

Picture yourself looking at a lighthouse directly in front of you, and feeling the need to walk toward and enter the lighthouse.

As you enter the door closes behind you making you feel very safe, (no one else can enter).

The room you enter is pure white with just a white chair and a shower, you instantly get undressed and go to the shower, once the control has been powered on, the water that comes cascading out is in beautiful rainbow colours, as you stand in the shower, feel those rainbow colours penetrating every pore of your skin and washing all of the grime of negativity.

When you have finished power off the shower, there is a big white fluffy gown with a hood hanging next to the shower; you put it on straight away. The gown will dry and protect you immediately.

You then head for a door over the other side of the room…. walk through the door now.

Housekeeping for the Soul

There is an inside corridor running around the lighthouse, starting with the first door, it opens and you walk inside the room, it is bright red in colour, feel the red being absorbed by the soles on your feet until it reaches your Root Chakra.

The door to the next room that you come to opens, you walk through and this room is orange in colour, feel the colour being absorbed through your feet until it has reached the Sacral Chakra, the place just below the naval.

The next door opens, as you walk through this room is bright yellow, feel the colour being absorbed through your feet as it reaches your Solar Plexus just above the naval.

The next door opens and as you walk through you see this room is emerald green, feel the colour being absorbed through your feet, the colour reaches your Heart Chakra, directly in the middle of the chest.

The door opens to the next room. This room is bathed in a light blue colour. You absorb this colour straight into your Throat Chakra. You head back into the corridor.

The door opens to the next room, this room is indigo colour, and you absorb this colour straight into your Third Eye Chakra.

The door opens to the very last of the seven chakras, this colour is purple, and you absorb the colour purple straight into your Crown Chakra, directly at the top of the head.

As you go through the last door, it takes you back in to the white room; you take off the fluffy gown and hang it back next to the shower, you walk toward the chair and put your clothes back on very quickly and leave the lighthouse via the door that you entered, the day is sunny and bright and you feel refreshed and renewed.

Please open your eyes.

Spiritual Awakening and the Symptoms

1. The feeling of very hot feet one minute and really cold feet the next, cold meaning ungrounded.
2. Having very vivid dreams bordering on nightmares.
3. Sleep patterns out of sync, waking up through the night.
4. Waves of emotion, being happy one day and then crying for no apparent reason the very next day.
5. Needing to let go of old stuff which is rising to the surface, feelings of being trapped.
6. Wanting to eat loads of food, craving junk foods, weight gain, or intolerances to certain foods.
7. Heightened senses, sensitive ears, ringing, buzzing, itching inside the ear, light sensitive.
8. Seeing orbs, glittery lights, shadows, auras around people, plants and objects.
9. Enhanced touch, taste smell.
10. Getting rid of toxins, through breakout of a rash.
11. Power surges, hot flushes, feeling chilled.

12. Confusion, forgetfulness.
13. Spiritual books, and teachers come your way.
14. Synchronicity, patterns.
15. Dizziness, brain fog.
16. Feelings of despair, irritability, anger.
17. Heart palpitations, pain or squeezing around the heart centre.
18. Feeling emotional, wanting to give and receive love.
19. Seeing spirit beings.
20. Aches and pains, joint pains, feeling lethargic.
21. The feeling of energy close at hand.

We all have a light that shines, and while some lights are a little brighter than others, just remember that your light will never die, but it can however become dull through lack of self-care through not looking after your inner self.

Ten Steps to Keeping Your Energy Safe.

1. Learn the Technique of Disconnection

To disconnect, see in your mind's eye a cord that may attach you to something, someone or a place and see this cord being cut, you will have given the intension to let go of that energy.

2. Clear Old Energy with Sage

Purchase from new age shop/online Californian White sage, the process is called smudging, light the sage and it will send smoke around the building, open all doors and windows, say an incantation to ask for all negative low energy to be taken from this building when done let the sage go out close all doors and windows and feel the energy change, (you can also sage yourself).

3. Use Crystals for Protection and Space Clearing

Crystals are vibration-use accordingly.

There are many crystals that can help with energy clearing, for universal love and for negativity, meanings for any crystal with specific energy clearing can be looked up online, in the search bar input 'gemstone Crystals properties', you can also purchase a book called the crystal bible or crystal prescriptions.

4. A Protection Cloak or Bubble

Placing a bubble of protection around you is easy. You are doing this with intention so remember there is no right or wrong way of doing this, if you struggle with visualisation don't worry as the thought and intention will facilitate the action, so in your mind's eye think of the colour that you love the most and place a long cloak with a hood over your psychical body, so just think of you and place this bubble or cloak all the way over you it's as easy as that, you will be protected until you decide to let the cloak or bubble fall away from you.

Of course it is also easy to let the cloak/bubble slip through negative intention so to keep up the shield let yourself believe it is in place.

5. A Healing of the Chakras

To heal the chakras is again done with intention and visualisation.

To bring a self-healing to the self, a good place to start is the chakras, always start with the head and work down the chakras have been made easy to repair through a colour system that was developed for use in healing techniques, there are many YouTube videos that will help with the cleansing, or find a therapist who can help with the balancing in a healing therapy.

6. Grounding

Grounding is very important. We need to stay grounded or we can feel nauseous, spaced out have cold feet and feel very dizzy, the grounding technique will help with focus and keep you safe.

Think of yourself as a tree and the souls of your feet have roots, with intention drive those roots far down into the ground that you stand on, best place outside on concrete or grass, with bare feet is good if at all possible but of course in a safe place. Once the roots have been planted you will feel much more earthed, this method needs to be done often.

You can also send all negative feelings to the earth, and down into the ground through your feet by intending the energy to travel through your physical body into the ground.

7. Closing Down Technique

So many people are open to the Spirit world; staying open day and night can make you feel very headachy and anxious.

There are many ways to close down starting with the chakras, starting with the root chakra, this energy point will need to stay slightly open as this keeps you grounded at all times.

So visualise your root chakra as a waterlily and see it closing but not fully closed, then work your way upward. Sacral, Solar Plexus, Heart, Throat, and Third Eye.

You then reach the crown chakra, this will need to be closed fully and see a door closing on this one, you have successfully closed down.

8. Cord Cutting

Cutting cords of fear is an amazing way of clearing old energy.

These cords are nothing but worry and fear feel with intention through your mind's eye hold a pair of scissors or knife cutting through the cords that attach you to someone or something, this is purely an emotional and mental exercise it will help you to let go of worry and fear based stress.

9. White Light Protection

With the intention of asking for Protection on the highest level. Asking the highest of source energy, or angelic to protect you in its purest form, on a daily basis ask for the white light protection this will facilitate protection from the spiritual realm into the physical body.

10. Controlling your Aura

The ability to bring your Aura in. So as not to give so much of yourself away, your Aura can shrink or be pulled in to the self for protection.

Lightly press your middle finger and thumb together, cross your arms, then cross your legs, this will pull your energy field closer to you, this will help when there are unwanted energies around that you wish not to feel.

If you have a problem crossing your legs then cross your ankles together, the whole process helps you to sit in energy that can be negative.

Affirmations

Affirmations can be part of the self-care daily routine in which our lives take on the rigours of every day rubbish. Using a few spoken words of wisdom can and will bring good health, prosperity, and for most even happiness. If we firmly believe in something then that something can and will work for us.

I have written a few affirmations to help you get started with your well-being and peace of mind. When we look after ourselves, we not only feel happier we feel healthier too.

But of course, you can also make up your own affirmations. Always remember to make them positive, no ifs or buts. These are negative words that seldom get recognised in the spirit world.

Affirmations

1. When I let go of past, the present is my future.
2. I am part of this earth; I am me; I love myself enough to say no; I release all worry and allow myself to relax into a relaxed presence. I am calm and relaxed. I have a positive attitude to all of life's learning.

3. I will start this day, and allow my mind, my body, and my soul to relax, feel safe, and heal, I ask for healing white light to help heal all challenges in the self, as I grow stronger and healthier. I now feel healthier and more beautiful from the inside out.

4. I will allow my energy to bring the highest light in, to heal my soul and spirit, to become whole and with one.

5. I will let go of all negative vibration today and become more positive.

6. I allow myself to grieve for loss of work, relationship, or death. I take this time to feel, as this feeling brings the pain that I will be able to release.

7. I only allow light to come into my world today. I let go of all dark.

8. I will heal myself before and after every connection with negative energies picked up from people and places.

9. I give permission to love myself more with each passing day.

10. I allow more love to enter my life, and I send these positive vibrations to heal others.

Conclusion

It is my belief that we have a supreme being who exists in another other-worldly dimension. This being can be known as God or Source. There are many names for this energy; I like to call it Source of All, which sends us the purist of love.

It is also my belief that we have a dark energy, which is born of ego, the one negative that rules our lives. We can manifest pure negativity through our own imaginary thoughts, which can then become an energy, not a so called breathing energy, but the one where it has come to life through our bad intentions of our own making.

Low energy can also exist from the spirit world. Just because someone was a bad boy here on earth doesn't mean that they are going to change when they reach the next world. There are lessons here.

How we live our life on this earth plane is not down to people's mistakes, so stop blaming others for the way you lead your life. There is always a way ahead. There is always an answer, whichever way you look at a situation, whether it's spiritual or earthly, the answers will always come. You just need to ask the right person. It's time to take your life in your own hands and make it the best life ever. After all you are a spiritual being having a human existence. Make your life count.

Reiki Principles

I will let go of worry

I will let go of anger

I will do my work honestly

I will give thanks for my many blessings

I will be kind to every living thing

Client and Workshop Testimonials

"I first met Lorna when I went on the Spirit Guide course. She instantly made me feel welcome and completely at ease, not only with herself but with every member of the course. There was such a ease and friendliness to Lorna that we all instantly loved her. I've subsequently joined Lorna's circle and her guidance and support have been second to none. Lorna never fails to surprise me with the power of her gift and helps me to awaken my own abilities with her gentleness and encouragement. This woman is an Earth Angel. "

Min Bullingham, Professional Holistic Therapist, Cirencester (simplymobileholistictherapy.co.uk).

"I have known Lorna since 1973, that's a long time! Lorna hadn't opened up psychically back then, but I remember well how she was with people, outgoing, happy and always ready to listen. Fast forward to the present day. Lorna is a gifted psychic medium and a natural teacher. She is not one to let her ego get in the way when she's teaching. For Lorna, passing on information to others opening to spirit is as natural as teaching things to her own children. Lorna is also a Reiki Master and from my own experience, when I have a Reiki session with her, I open up to spirit and see some amazing things, far more than when I am simply meditating. On several occasions I have connected psychically with Lorna while she is working on my chakras. Lorna's teaching approach is all-inclusive, which means, pupils willing, that everyone gets to try taking the others in

the circle through a meditation, or to have a go at psychometry and many other things that we do. It's all very hands-on and it helps to build confidence as much as it helps to develop people's psychic abilities whatever they may be. My advice? If you feel a pull towards psychic development, give Lorna a call or email her. She is very approachable and her rates will not scare you!"

Paul King, Writer, Designer, Healer and more. May 2017

"Lorna is a lovely lady, always very welcoming who will put you at ease very quickly. I have had many readings. Whenever I am unsure of which path to follow Lorna will connect with my guardians and they will ask Lorna to show me the right way with the information they are passing through. It has all been very comforting. I have also received many Reiki treatments from Lorna and again she has put me at ease straight away and the feeling during and after a session is sometimes quite overwhelming. She has helped me identify many minor problems and helped to heal me. Lorna runs several classes some of which I have attended. I have found them all very informative and useful. I have been able to put so much of the information into practice which I believe has helped me become the person I am now. Lorna is a totally gifted lady and I am so pleased that our paths have crossed. I look forward to many more classes, treatments and readings."

Hayley S Swadling,
Professional Massage Therapist
at Butterfly Massage, Gloucester
(butterflymassage.co.uk)

*
"I was advised by a friend to attend one of Lorna's workshops. My friend showed me a picture of Lorna beforehand, as I can tell instantly what sort of person I will be coming into contact with. The photo showed that Lorna was a sensitive, kind, empathic person, and I knew that

everything would be ok. After my first workshop with Lorna, I booked a reading, as I was tying myself up in knots trying to decide which path to follow with my future career. Once I was settled in Lorna's delightful spiritual room, she instantly picked up the spirits of my parents, and described them to me perfectly. We discussed everything on my mind (and more), and I came away feeling that I was going in the right direction, and that my spiritual family were in fact in the loop. Lorna will always be honest with you, even if the advice given is not something you are expecting to hear. This is the best way, as it shows what we need to know, rather than what we think we want to know, and the spirits deliver this through Lorna to help us to grow in the most amazing way."

*Cassie Martin, Angel Reiki Therapist
and Psychic Medium in training,
Forest Of Dean, Gloucestershire*

"I have known Lorna for more than 5 years. She is a very good Reiki healer and I always feel so much better for weeks after receiving Reiki from her. I have sat in circle with her for over 3 years. She has taught me so much. It is always lovely to go to circle where she makes us all feel welcome and helps each of us in different ways. I find her to be a wonderful teacher and would recommend anyone to attend her courses. She has a natural way about her that makes it easy to understand her teaching. From connecting to spirit, to psychometry, she explains everything so well. I feel I have gained a lot from Lorna and have greatly improved my psychic abilities thanks to her."

*Ann Loy-Williams, Reiki Channel
and Psychic Medium in training, Gloucester*

"I stumbled across Lorna by some miracle and have no idea how I came to find her on Facebook. I can only believe spirit was guiding me in her direction. After leaving a previous circle, I was looking for further development and support on my psychic pathway and was pleased to be invited to join Lorna's closed weekly circle. Lorna is a powerhouse of

knowledge and inspiration and instantly made me feel at ease in her company. Supporting me through her powerful Reiki healing and guidance through circle, I feel I have come on in leaps and bounds. She has such a warm friendly approach to anyone wanting to learn or those who are seeking support after the loss of a loved one, through her psychic readings. She has encouraged me to face fears that were holding me back, and is a great sounding board when I have been feeling tender as my spiritual journey unfolds. Attending her psychic development workshop, I like the way she brings humour into awakening our psychic senses, and does everything she can to make everyone feel safe and at home. An amazing woman with a huge heart.

Kelly Martin, Author of
'When Everyone Shines But You' (Book 1),
When Everyone Shines Including You (Book 2)
Gloucester
(kellymartin.co.uk)

About Me

I am firstly a mum, a grandma, and a great grandma. My family always come first, they are my life.

Then came the turning on of the lights or should I say my light. It took a long while for me to understand what was going on, but through development the switch went on full blast. I couldn't stop what was happening and through trials and tribulations it came together.

I started giving readings, but something was missing from my life. This is when I started to listen to my inner guidance and learned Reiki to the Master/Teacher level. I love to channel Reiki healing energy. Through this I am able to help people who may be struggling on different levels and need some additional human and spiritual support.

I love every minute of being in contact with Spirit. My guides have been very welcoming, and have taught me a lot during my education, and although I teach everything they have set out to teach me, I have never regretted any of the learning.

I have been married for 40 years, and I am a mother to two sons and two daughters, a grandmother to five grandchildren, and a great grandmother to one. Family life keeps me human and down-to-earth.

I also have a very boisterous dog called Merlin who loves to keep circle members entertained and grounded. He is also partial to stealing home-made biscuits at the end of the night. Cheeky chappy is Merlin!

My husband keeps me grounded as my mystical side is very different from what he believes, but that is what makes life fun, our differences and our similarities.

Who said being a supernatural channel for the 'other side' was meant to be easy? I am constantly growing and learning, and spirit is always challenging me to expand my knowledge and understanding.

I am glad I stepped into this magic carpet ride because my life is fulfilling as a result.

Contact details:

Email: PsychicLorna@Yahoo.co.uk
Website: www.RayofLight-Teachings.co.uk
Facebook: RayofLightSpiritualTeachings
Twitter: https://twitter.com/Psychiclorna

Excerpt from Chapter One of Book One by Lorna Hedges:

'From Housewife to Psychic, Awakening Your Sixth Sense'

ISBN-13: 978-1533497505
ISBN-10: 1533497508

The Beginning

Strange, because I never saw this coming!

We are tested time and again throughout this life journey, yet the biggest difficulty we have is that we hang onto all our fears. This comes from the countless years of growing up with indoctrination from our parents, our teachers, authority figures and society in general, as well as from our own experiences.

Our lives could be so much happier and more settled if we followed the guidance of our hearts, living our lives with compassion and gratitude. Finding the true self will find the real person, the spiritual part of us, the Self. The love that is deep inside has been repressed by those who live within their own fears and doubts.

The biggest lesson I have learned is that letting go of all that's not needed is so very hard. Allowing the self to dwell on the negative will ensure that the negative will just keep taking over our lives. This is the ego in action, the part of us that is the negative, the fixation that tells you in your head not to do something that is important to you; the fixation that will make you stay in the negative within the fears.

It's not so easy to stay focused on the positive. I've found that after many years of following the path of ego, with a large modicum of negative, it took a monumental shift in my life to become a more positive person by following my heart more. This is what brought me to this place in my life, the emergence of the spiritual Self - the person I was always meant to be.

From the beginning to the end of my learning it has been my pain, but also my pleasure, that has taken me to this stage in my spiritual development, which has been, and still is, hard work.

71897171R00076

Made in the USA
Columbia, SC
07 June 2017